29 COWBOY PATTERNS FOR CARVERS

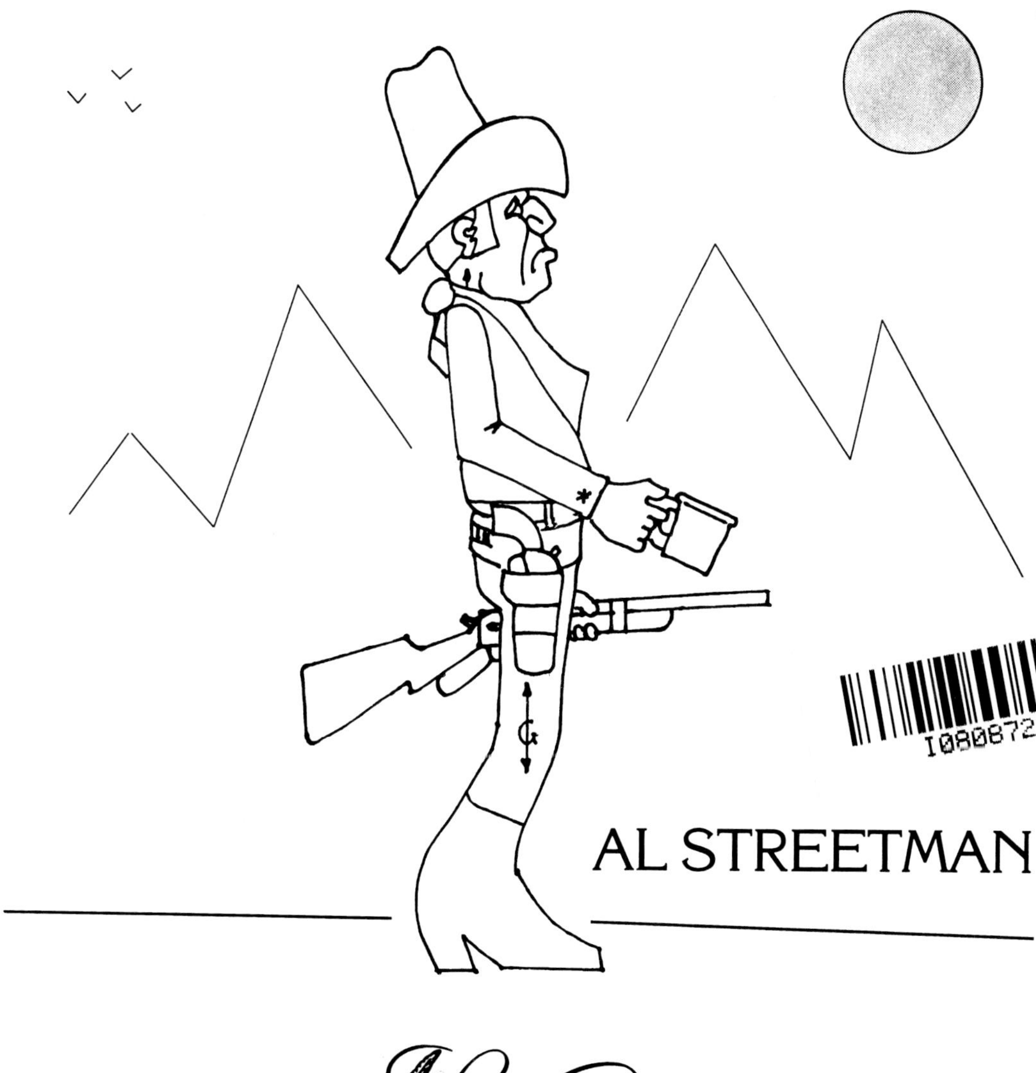

AL STREETMAN

Schiffer Publishing Ltd

77 Lower Valley Road, Atglen, PA 19310

Dedication

To "Brucie" Kuhlmann, for your support and encouragement in general, and for your friendship in particular.

Acknowledgments

The following people helped make this book possible. I thank you all.

Marilynn Jones: For your continued word-processing support, both in data entry, and especially in data retrieval.

Jody Garrett, Woodcraft Supply Corp.: For all the help you give to us "starving artists," and for providing us with various carving tool samples for evaluation and consideration.

Delta Technical Coatings, Inc.: The paint samples were excellent, and satisfactory in all respects.

Woodcraft Supply Corp.; Parkersburg, West Virginia: Excellent carving tools and supplies.

Royal Brush Mfg.,Inc.: Excellent quality paintbrushes at an affordable price.

Library of Congress Catalog Card Number: 96-70625

Printed in China
ISBN: 0-7643-0187-X

Book Layout by Michael William Potts

Published by Schiffer Publishing Ltd.
77 Lower Valley Road
Atglen, PA 19310
Phone: (610) 593-1777 Fax: (610) 593-2002

Please write for a free catalog.
This book may be purchased from the publisher.
Please include $2.95 for shipping.
Try your bookstore first.

We are interested in hearing from authors
with book ideas on related subjects.

Contents

Introduction

Even in this modern age cowboys and the "old West" still capture our hearts and imaginations. In response to the many phone calls and letters requesting more cowboy patterns, this book is for you, and for anyone else who wants to create some of these lovable characters. Once you escape the confines of the city, things like the "Information Superhighway" just don't seem to matter. Sitting atop your trusty horse with the wind of freedom blowing through your hair, and miles of open country staring back at you, you know that this is how life was meant to be lived. The cowboy was, and still is to some extent, the epitome of this carefree existence. In general, cowboys work hard when there is work to be done, and play hard when the work is over. With few exceptions, they are known and remembered as being honorable and loyal.

My favorite pattern in this book, the fence sitter, is one of those exceptions. He is honorable and loyal, but I think he falls a bit short of being a hard worker. In fact, I think the hardest work he does each day is to climb up on the fence, so that he may observe how work is performed. You will find one of these characters on every ranch. Although they aren't worth the powder it would take to blow them into next Sunday, they are likeable fellas, and probably serve some real purpose in life's great scheme. (We just haven't figured out yet what that real purpose is).

The cowboys in this book are carved using the same techniques I presented and used in my **Western Gunfighter** carving book. This book is for those of you who already possess basic carving skills, but need some patterns to practice those skills on. If any special notes are required, they are included on that particular pattern.

The patterns in this book include approximate dimensions of the side and front views, if you wish to carve them the same size as I originally designed them. If you desire a larger or smaller version, simply enlarge or shrink the pattern on a photocopying machine. You may also want to use the photocopying machine to make several sizes of the hand template. This way you will be sure to have a hand outline that is the proper size for the cowboy you carve.

You will notice that the patterns contain several drawings: a side and front profile with dimensions, which is the pattern you will use to saw out the body blank; a head pattern, and accessories in many instances, depending on the pattern you are going to carve. The numbers on the arms of the patterns correspond to numbers on the hand template, and are the suggested hands to use for that pattern. If you would rather use different hands, feel free to do so. This will allow you to achieve many different looks from just a few patterns. Each pattern also shows some assembled views of the pieces, so you can picture how the head, body, and accessories might look if you desire to carve that pattern.

I use Basswood whenever possible, but any soft wood such as Jelutong, clear Spruce, or Sugar/White Pine will work equally well. If possible, use a bandsaw with a 1/8" blade to cut out the side and front profiles. (On the patterns with extended arms, you may choose to saw out the arms separately, so as to make maximum use of the wood grain direction, then attach them to the body before doing your final carving). The bandsaw will allow you to release the rough version of the cowboy from the block of wood faster than trying to use a coping saw or other means to cut out the pattern.

GENERAL NOTES

1. Trace the head and body pattern, or make a copy of it on a photocopying machine. Glue the pattern you copied or traced onto some heavy paper such as poster paper or a manila file folder. When the glue is dry, cut out the pattern. This method will prevent you from ruining the master patterns in your book.

2. Lay your pattern on the wood, trace the outline of it, and saw it out.

3. You should now have a rough blank ready to be carved.

4. Use your own techniques and style to bring the carving to the finished stage.

5. You will notice that some of the patterns to be used for sawing out the body do not show hands attached. This method allows you to carve the body, then decide on the size and style of hands you want to use for that carving. (This is where you will put the hand template to work). Many times the type of hands will be determined by what accessories you are going to include with the carving (rifle, coffee cup, etc) . Because you are carving the hands separately from the body, you can orient them to take advantage of the wood grain when you saw them out. This will allow you endless variations of hand positions, so you can give more life to your carvings. Also, if you are creating an extreme caricature, you can use a larger than normal hand pattern to add more humor to the carving.

6. I recommend carving the head separately from the main body. This gives you several advantages: (1) if you make a mistake on the head or body, the other part won't be ruined ; (2) you can assemble the head to the body looking straight ahead, or you can turn it to one side (turning the head to one side will give more "life" to your carvings); (3) You can "mix and match" different heads with different bodies, therefore gaining more variations from a given number of patterns.

7. If you carve the pistols, rifles, and other accessories as separate pieces you can orient them to get maximum strength from the grain direction, and this also gives you more flexibility in positioning them on the body.

CARVING TOOLS

For those of you who may want to duplicate the cuts I make using the same tools as I use, I have listed below the tools used in my cowboy carving projects.

1/8" V gouge - Hair details, seam separations
1/4" V gouge - Seam separations, wrinkles in clothes
2mm #11 U gouge - Large hair details, minor scooping
3mm #11 U gouge - Large hair details, minor scooping
5mm #3 Flat gouge - Wood removal in restricted areas
8mm #2 Flat gouge - Wood removal in large areas
10mm #7 U gouge - Scooping wood from hat brims
4mm #8 U gouge - Scooping wood from hat brims in small areas
Fixed blade (Bütz) carving and detail knives - General wood removal and details such as eye carving.

TIPS

1. Eyes

A. **QUILT PIN METHOD:** I often use various sizes of plastic-head quilting pins to make eyes. Mark where you want the eyes to be on the finished carving. Using a drill and bit that is slightly larger than the pin head you are going to use, make a hole for each eye.

Using wire cutters, snip off the pin head, leaving about 1/4" of the pin attached to the head.

Insert the pin head into the eye socket, with the pin end going in first. Use a nail set to seat the head into the hole until only a small orb protrudes. This gives a fairly realistic eye without causing too much effort on your part. For extra detail, remove a triangular-shaped piece of wood from the sides of the pin head. This will make a very realistic eye when it is painted.

B. **PUNCH METHOD:** A second way to create eyes the easy way is to use carver's eye punches. Select the size eye punch you want to use, based on the size of the eye sockets you have made. Push the eye punch against the socket firmly and rotate it. After making both eyes, remove triangular-shaped pieces of wood from the corners to give more detail. Use your knife, if necessary, to smooth and round off the eyeball.

C. **FOOTBALL METHOD:** A more realistic way to make eyes is to first carve the eye sockets so that about a 90° angle is formed. Lightly sketch in a football-shaped eye in each socket, such that the top half of the football is on the upper half of the socket, and the lower half of the football is on the lower half of the socket. When you sketch in the footballs, make the outside ends lower than the inside ends. Using the tip of your knife, score the football outline to a depth of about 1/16". Now use the tip of your knife to remove triangular-shaped pieces of wood from the left and right corner of each eye. This will leave a small section of wood inside each football, which will be the eyeball. use your knife to round off and smooth the eyeball. You can vary the way you remove the triangular-shaped corners, if you want the eyes to be looking more to one side, rather than straight ahead.

D. **MOUND METHOD:** The most realistic way to make eyes is to first rough carve the nose so it is standing out from the face. Next, sketch a circle or oval on each side of the nose to represent where the eye mounds will be located. Using a smaller "V" gouge such as a 1/8" size, or your knife tip, go around the circles or ovals so the mounds will be defined, and separated from the face area. Use your knife to round the sharp edges of the mounds, and the face area around the mounds.

Divide the mounds into thirds by sketching two curved horizontal lines across each one, making sure that the lines join at each corner of the mound.(Look at your own eyes in a mirror to see what I mean here). Using your knife tip, score each horizontal line about 1/16" deep. Working from the **center** of the eye mound, use your knife tip to shave **upward** toward the top horizontal line, and **downward** toward the bottom horizontal line. This will make the eyelids stand out from the eyeball area. Finally, remove small triangular pieces of wood from each corner of the eye, so the eyeball will be rounded from left to right, as well as top to bottom.

Changing the size and shape of the mounds, and the spacing between the horizontal lines, will allow you to achieve many effects and expressions on your carvings.

One last thing concerning eyes: Don't get upset if you discover that you have carved one eye smaller or at a different angle than the other eye. This "accident" may work to your advantage. It will lend an interesting variation to the carving, and no one has to know you didn't do it that way on purpose!!

2. Buying Wood

When buying wood, whether it be Basswood, Spruce, or some other type, try to pick the **lightest** pieces. They tend to have less fat and sap in them, so they are **easier** to carve.

3. Thickness of Wood

I normally use the same thickness of wood for the head as I use for the body. This provides plenty of wood for a big floppy hat brim.

4. Making a Rifle

If making a rifle for your carving, it is easier and more realistic if you make the barrel separate from the stock. The best material for the barrel is 1/16" aluminum tubing which can be purchased at any hobby or hardware store. To cut it to length, simply roll it lightly back and forth under your knife blade. It is a soft metal and won't hurt your knife edge. After carving the wood stock, a small amount of cement such as Ambroid or DuPont will hold the barrel firmly in place. An alternate method for the barrel is to use a section of 1/8" wood dowel, glued in place and painted Silver.

5. 5 O'clock Shadow

If you want your cowboy to have a "scruffy" look, rather than a well-manicured look, you may want to add some beard stubble to the cheek, chin and neck areas. This may be done by pricking small pieces of wood loose using a very tiny "V" gouge (such as a **2mm #39** gouge), or by making small indentations in the wood using the sharpened tip of a small finishing nail or electric engraving tool. An alternate method, if you prefer, is to add the stubble detail using a burning device such as a Hot Tool, Detail Master, etc.

After painting the flesh and hair color, very lightly dry-brush a small amount of Black onto the beard stubble area, to give that 5 o'clock shadow look. If you have painted the hair Gray or White to depict an old grizzly cowboy, you may want to dry-brush small amounts of Black and Gray onto the beard stubble area.

6. A Long Day on the Trail

If you want your cowboy to have a dusty, trail-worn appearance, *lightly* dry-brush **small** amounts of Gray or White paint all over the carving. This will help remove the "new" look from his clothing and accessories.

7. Wrinkles and Folds

An easy way to help determine where you want to place some wrinkles and folds in the arms, torso and legs is to observe and note where the wood grain changes direction as you are carving. Usually in the crook of an elbow or behind the knees, you will notice that wood "fuzzies" try to appear, no matter how carefully you carve or how sharp your knife is. That is because the wood grain direction is changing, and in one direction or the other, you are trying to carve against the grain, thus the "fuzzies" appear. These spots are perfect candidates for wrinkles and folds, made with a large "V" tool or by cutting wedges out with your knife. As a beginning carver, if you do nothing more than add a few cuts in these areas, you will be amazed at the difference in the way the carving looks. With experience, you will start noticing other places to add wrinkles and folds.

8. Changing Pattern Sizes

For those of you who have never had much practice enlarging or reducing patterns, or being able to calculate how much enlargement or reduction you need to select on the photocopying machine, here are some general guidelines:

Let's say you have a pattern that shows a side profile requiring 2" thick wood, and you want to make the pattern larger so it will fit on 3" thick wood. Use the following formula to calculate what percentage enlargement to select on the copier:

[New Dimension Desired ÷ Present Dimension] x 100
= % to select on copier machine.

Using our example, this would work out as follows:

[3" ÷ 2"] x100 = **150 %**.

Going the other way, let's say you have a pattern that shows a 2" side profile, and you want to reduce it down so it will fit on a piece of 1-3/4" thick wood. Using the same formula, it works out as follows:

[1.75" ÷ 2"] x100 = **87.5 %**.

If the machine you are using won't cut large enough or small enough to get the job done on the first try, additional steps may be required. Go ahead and make your first copy using the largest enlargement or reduction setting you can select. Measure the **new** dimensions on your *copy,* **(which will now be your Present Dimension)**, then use the same formula as before to calculate how much additional enlargement or reduction is needed to get the pattern to the size you desired it to be.

9. A Hint for Hands

When making separate hands that are going to be holding some object such as a rifle, it is easiest if you first cut out the top profile of the hand, drill a hole large enough for the object to fit through, then saw out the side profile of the hand. This procedure will help prevent the hand from splitting when you drill it.

10. Oh Those Legs!

On the patterns where the legs are together, rather than spread apart, you may want to separate them slightly by sawing on a line from the bottom of the feet, up to where the crotch would be. You can do this with your bandsaw, or a coping saw. This line will help you keep the legs symmetrical and centered on the body.

11. Easy Rope

An easy way to make "rope" is to use heavy cotton twine. Cut a section of twine, soak it in a thinned-down solution of brown stain or paint, and let it dry. After it is dry, you can position it in the character's hands, loop it around his head, or position it as you desire.

12. Barbed Wire

To make "barbed-wire" fast and easy, obtain a roll of small-gauge wire from the hardware store. Cut a section of wire about 6' in length, and fold it in half. Hook the loop end around a nail and clamp the nail in a vise. Insert the two loose ends in an electric drill, chuck them securely, and slowly activate the drill so the wire twists tightly. Remove the ends from the drill and secure them so that the wire remains stretched out and firm. Now using small sections of wire, wrap each section around the main wire several times, to form the "barbs". Space the barbs about 3/8" apart on the main wire.

13. Fence Posts

The most realistic fence posts can be achieved by using small twigs, which have a natural weathered look. If you are unable to obtain twigs, small wooden dowels may be substituted.

14. Wire Reels

Wire reels for wrapping barbed-wire around may be constructed using sections of wooden dowel as the hub, and thin sections of scrap wood as the cross-pieces on the ends.

15. Chuck Wagon Utensils

To give coffee pots, cups and plates that old fashioned "enameled" look, paint them with a base coat of WHITE. After the base coat is dry, use a piece of old sponge, and lightly dab BLUE or BLACK over the WHITE.

16. A Cup & Saucer Alternative

Many times, you can find plates, cups, coffee pots and other accessories which are the right size for your project at stores which carry doll and doll-house supplies.

17. Hands

For those patterns where the hands are to be carved separately, the following instructions may be used if you are not familiar with this method of hand carving:

(A) Lay out the top view of the hands on a piece of 3/4" thick basswood. Leave a short section of wood at the rear of each hand when you lay out the pattern. This section will serve as a handle while you carve and shape the hands, and will form the wrist pegs in a later step. Saw out the top profile of the hands.

(B) Now, using the top set of hands in the Hand Studies as a reference, sketch in the side profile of the hands, then saw them out. You now should have two hands that will require very little work to finish.

(C) Sketch in the thumbs. Remove wood from each hand using a knife or a **#7 10mm "U" gouge**, so the thumbs are well-defined, then round off the sharp edges of the thumbs.

(D) Draw a line in the middle of the finger section to divide it in half. Now draw lines to divide each of these sections in half. You should now have four fingers defined, all approximately equal.

(E) Using a **1/8" "V" gouge**, go over these lines so the fingers will be separated. As an option, to add further detail without too much pain on your part, use a bandsaw, scroll saw or coping saw to carefully saw along these lines. Use your knife to remove any fuzzy wood caused by the saw cuts, and to remove any sharp edges still remaining on the hands. At this point, if you do nothing else, you will have two hands that will look perfectly good once they are painted. Experienced carvers may add more detailing as they desire, such as knuckles and wrinkles on the finger joints.

(F) Using your knife, trim down the sections of wood protruding from the rear of the hands, so as to form a "wrist" or "pin" that will fit snugly into the holes you drilled earlier in the arms. When done properly, the hand should appear to be coming out of the sleeve. This method allows you to turn the hands in various directions, so your carvings will appear more lifelike.

General Painting Suggestions For All Cowboys In This Book

I have included some suggested colors and paint brushes for all patterns. If you have a preference for a different color scheme, by all means use it. After all, it's your cowboy, and you can dress him any way you desire.

I have also listed the colors produced by Delta Technical Coatings, Inc. and their identification numbers, which I have found to be suitable for painting these carvings. I have used these colors, and the results were excellent. I hope this will help minimize your confusion when trying to sort through the maze of paint brands and colors at your hobby or craft store.

White #2505 - Eyes, dots on bandannas, hair
Sandstone #2402 - Hats, hair
Antique White #2001 - Cigarettes
Black #2506 - Eye dots, ash on cigarettes, hats, shirts
Charcoal #2436 - Hats, ash on cigarettes, 5 o'clock shadows
Fleshtone #2019 - Face, hands, other skin areas
Burnt Sienna #2030 - Boots, gunbelts, any other leather items
Burnt Umber #2025 - Hats, pants
Walnut #2024 - Gun handles, any other wooden items
Blue Heaven #2037 - Eye dots, shirts
Crocus Yellow #2459 - Dots on bandannas
Denim Blue #2477 - Pants, shirts
Crimson #2076 - Bandannas, shirts
Navy Blue #2089 - Shirts, pants, bandannas
Quaker Grey #2057 - Hats, pants, hair
Silver #2603 - Metal items
Red Iron Oxide #2020 - Boots, other leather items
Territorial Beige #2425 - Hats, shirts, pants
Cadet Gray #2426 - Hats, ash on cigarettes
Autumn Brown #2055 - Hats, pants
GP Purple #2091 - Shirts
Pigskin #2093 - Hats, shirts
Trail Tan #2435 - Hats, shirts, pants
Palomino Tan #2108 - Hats, shirts, pants
Lilac Dusk #2403 - Shirts
Persimmon #2480 - "Wind" burning on face, other flesh areas

Warm Brown Antiquing Gel - "Aging" the finished carving
Clear Satin Varnish - Sealing the finished carving

The best paintbrushes I have found, for the money, are made by the Royal Brush Mfg. Company. They come in a wide assortment of sizes and shapes, are durable, and most important are affordable. In general, here are the ones I use and recommend for painting your carvings:

Details such as eyes, other small areas:
Series 250, #0 and #00
Large areas: **Series 170**, #2 and #4
Details in large areas: **Series 180**, #6
Blending, "weathering": **Series 150**, #2, #4
Series 250 are round detail brushes.
Series 170 are Cat Tongues (Filberts)
Series 180 are Triangular
Series 150 are Flat Shaders

You may have heard and read this a million times, but when painting your carvings, keep the word **THIN** in mind. What you want to do is stain the wood to give it some color and life, but you don't want the paint so thick that it covers up the beauty of the wood. **NOTE:** When painting the head and hands, I generally use a little thicker mixture of paint than I use on the rest of the carving. I want the face to be a bit more intense than the rest of the carving, since the head and face is what sets most of the mood for the carving.

"Antiquing" the Project

Once the paint is dry, you may want to "age" your cowboys with an antiquing product in order to help tone down the colors a bit. I have had excellent results using antiquing gels made by Delta Technical Coatings. These are available at hobby and craft stores. They come in various colors, so you can create different effects.

Brush a coat of antiquing gel on the carving, then wipe it off using a damp rag or sponge. It is your option how much you wipe off. After the antiquing is dry, I like to finish my carvings with a coat of brush-on acrylic varnish. Delta Technical Coatings also makes an excellent varnish. I prefer the one that leaves a Satin finish. This particular finish is not too flat nor too glossy, but leaves a "soft" look to the completed carving. **(I usually put a coat of varnish on the face, hands and hair area BEFORE I antique the carving).** This will prevent these areas from absorbing too much antiquing color.

A Final Note

I hope that in some way I have been able to help each of you with some aspect of carving and painting. When we share tips and information, we all become better. If you have any comments or questions about something in this book, or if you have an idea you'd like to see me put in a future book, please feel free to write or call me at the following address and telephone number. I welcome any comments or suggestions you have.

Al Streetman
1609 N. Fordson Drive
Oklahoma City, Ok. 73127
(405) 495-0816

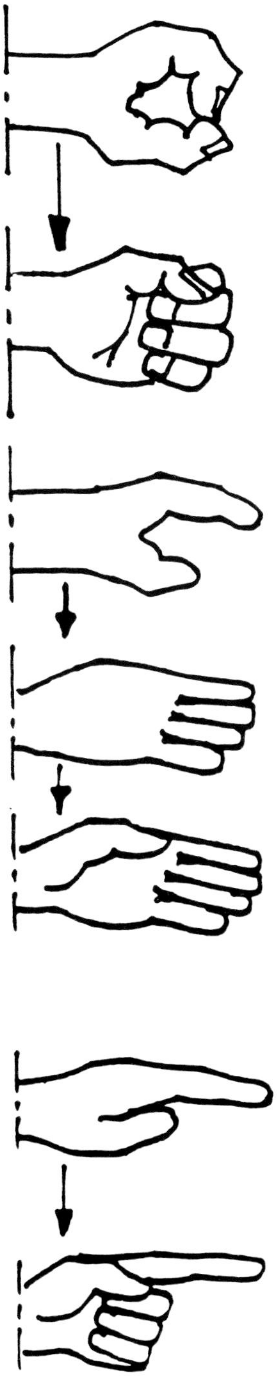

HAND STUDIES

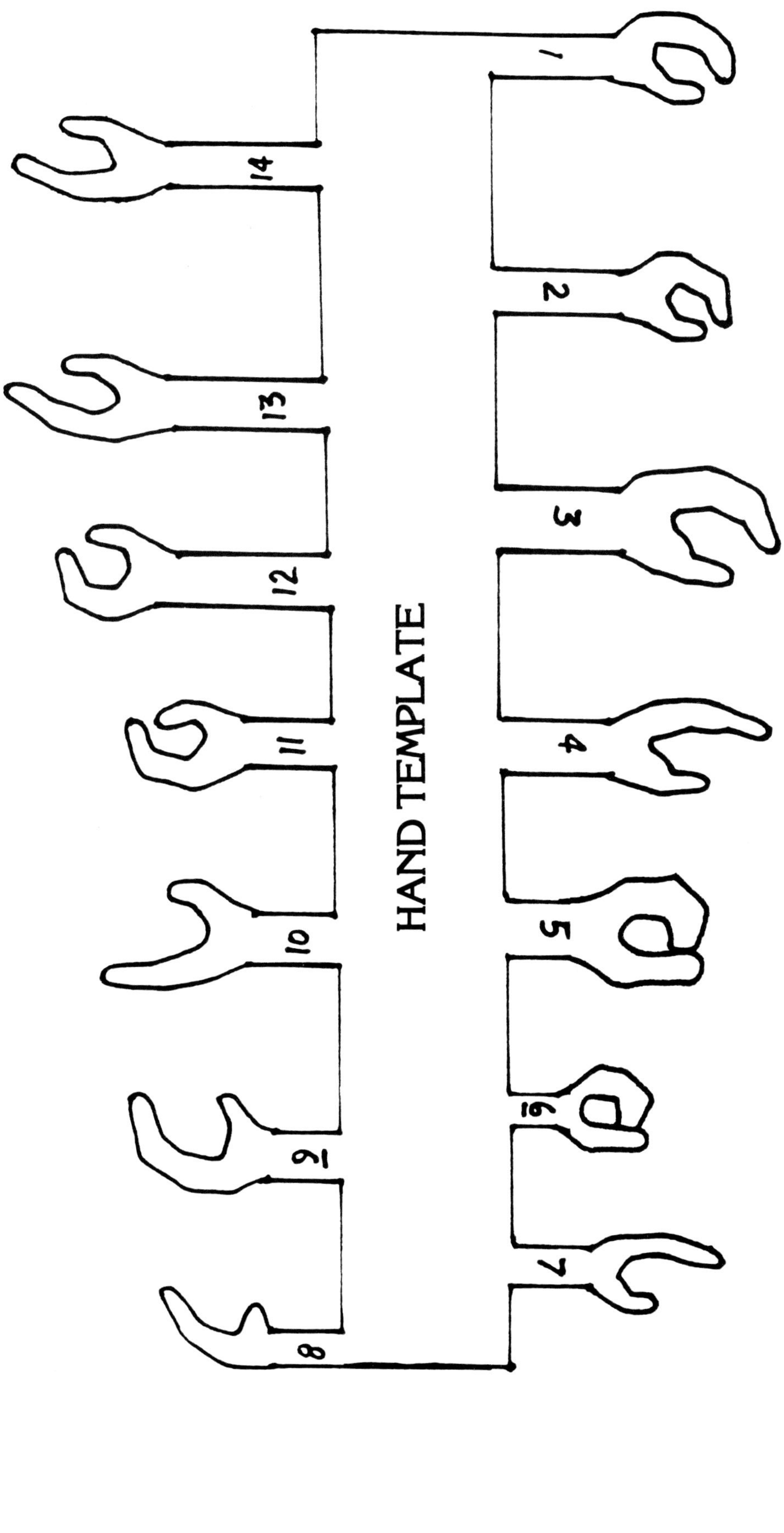

Fence Sitter #1

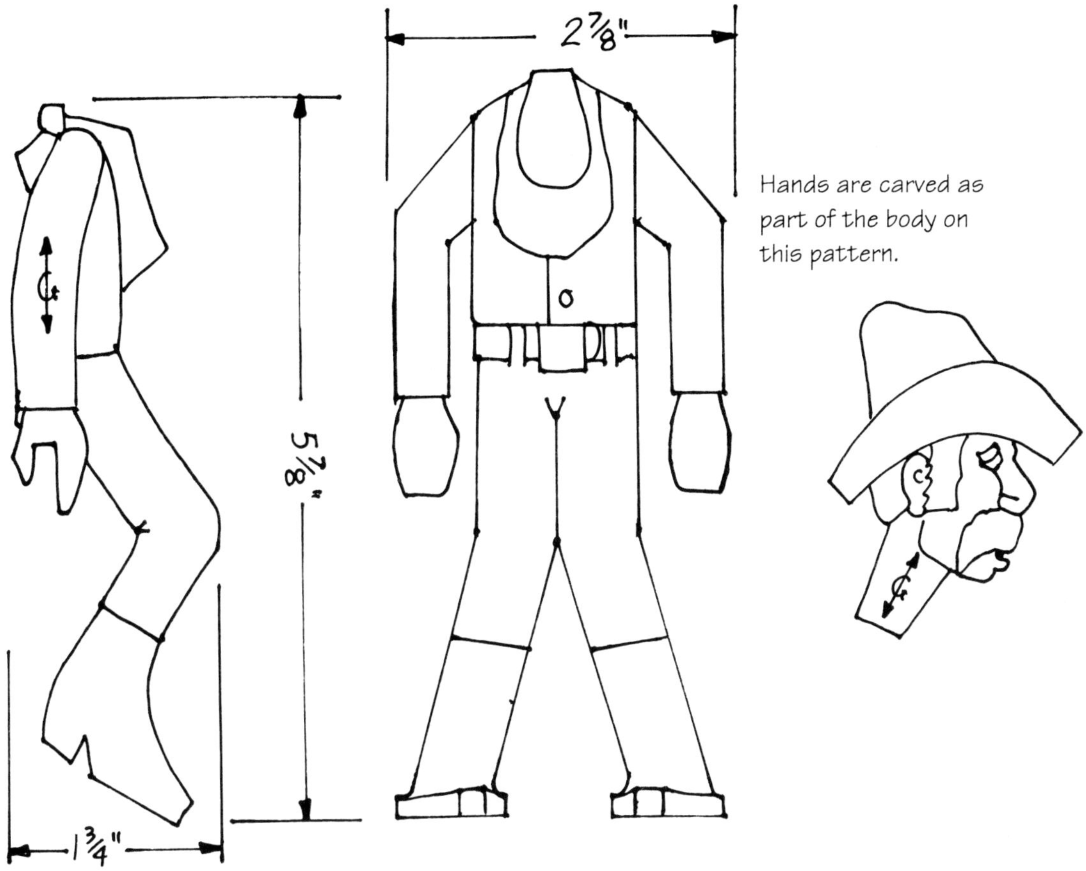

Fence Sitter #2

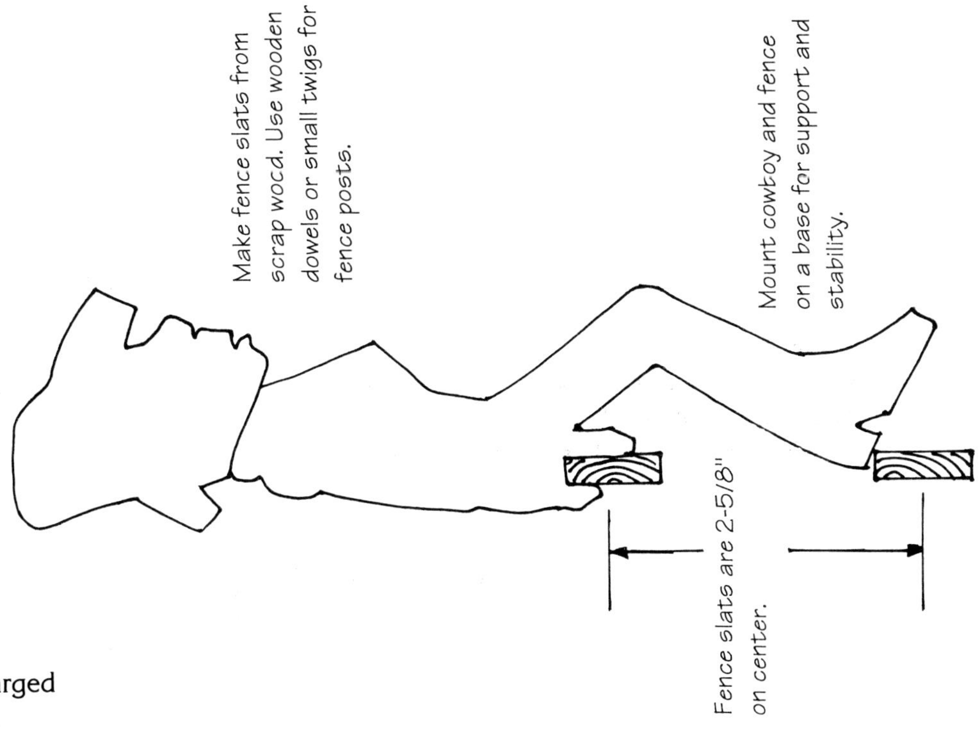

This page must be enlarged 135% for original size.

RODEO PRACTICE #1

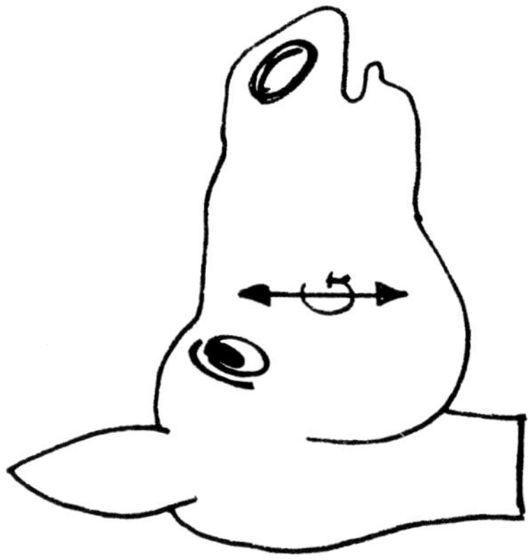

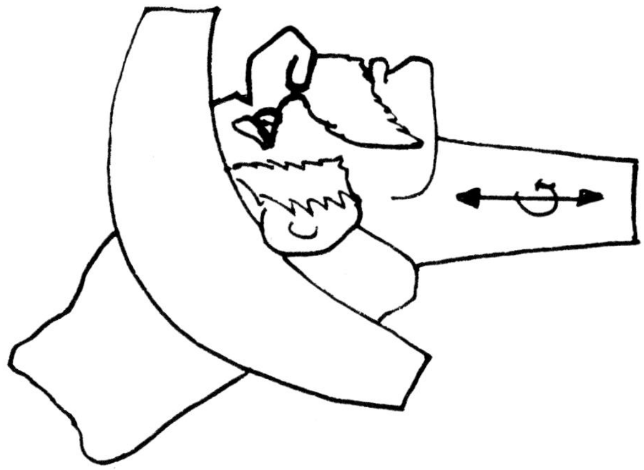

Horse head is sawn from 3/4" thick wood.

Drill 1/8" holes in ends of arms for insertion of hands.

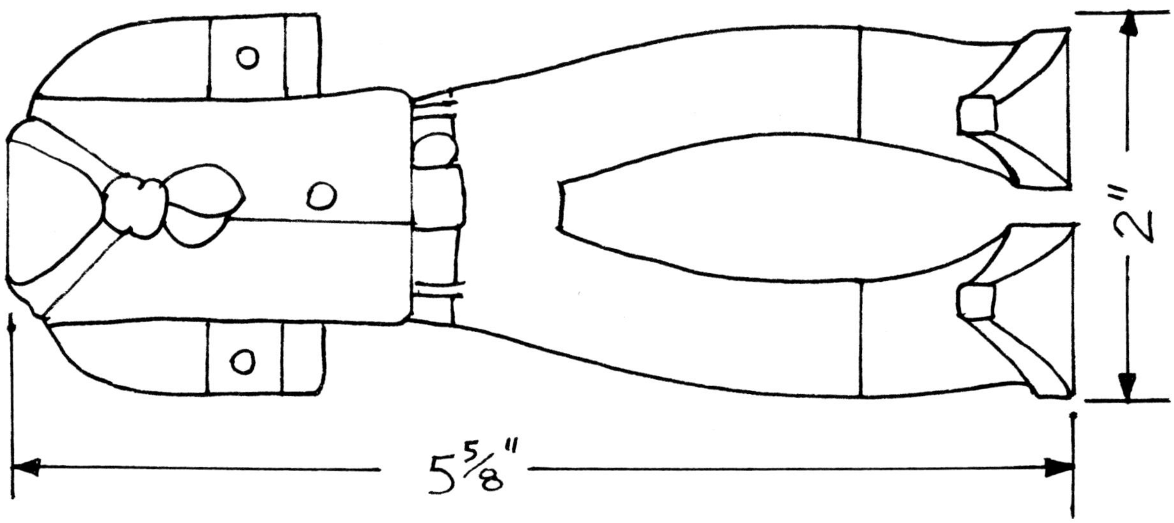

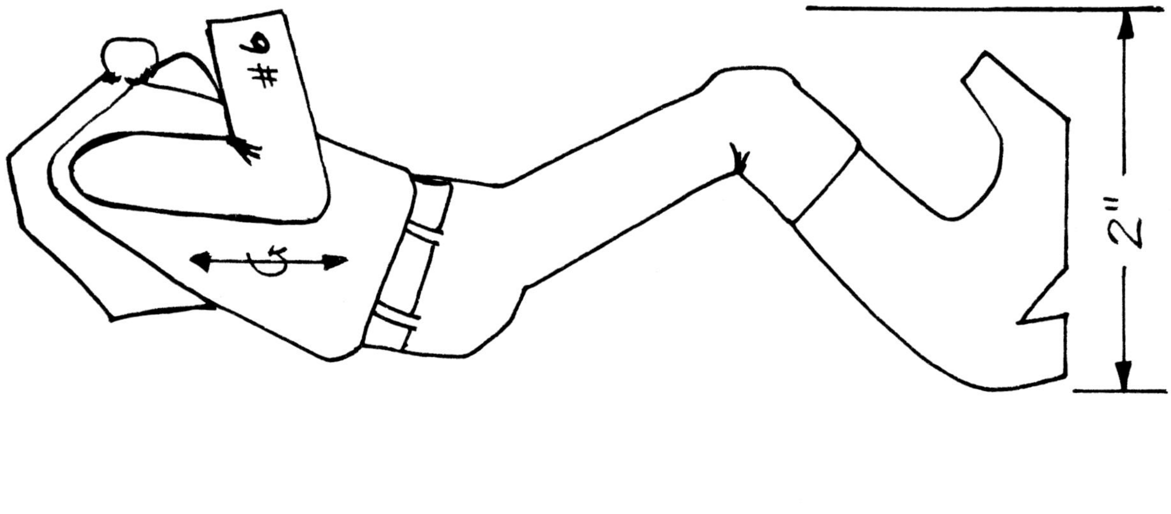

Rodeo Practice #2

Reins are made from heavy twine or similar.
Loop around nose of horse, run across
top of head, and down through 3/16" holes in hands.
Let a small amount hang down below the hands, and cut
off the excess length.

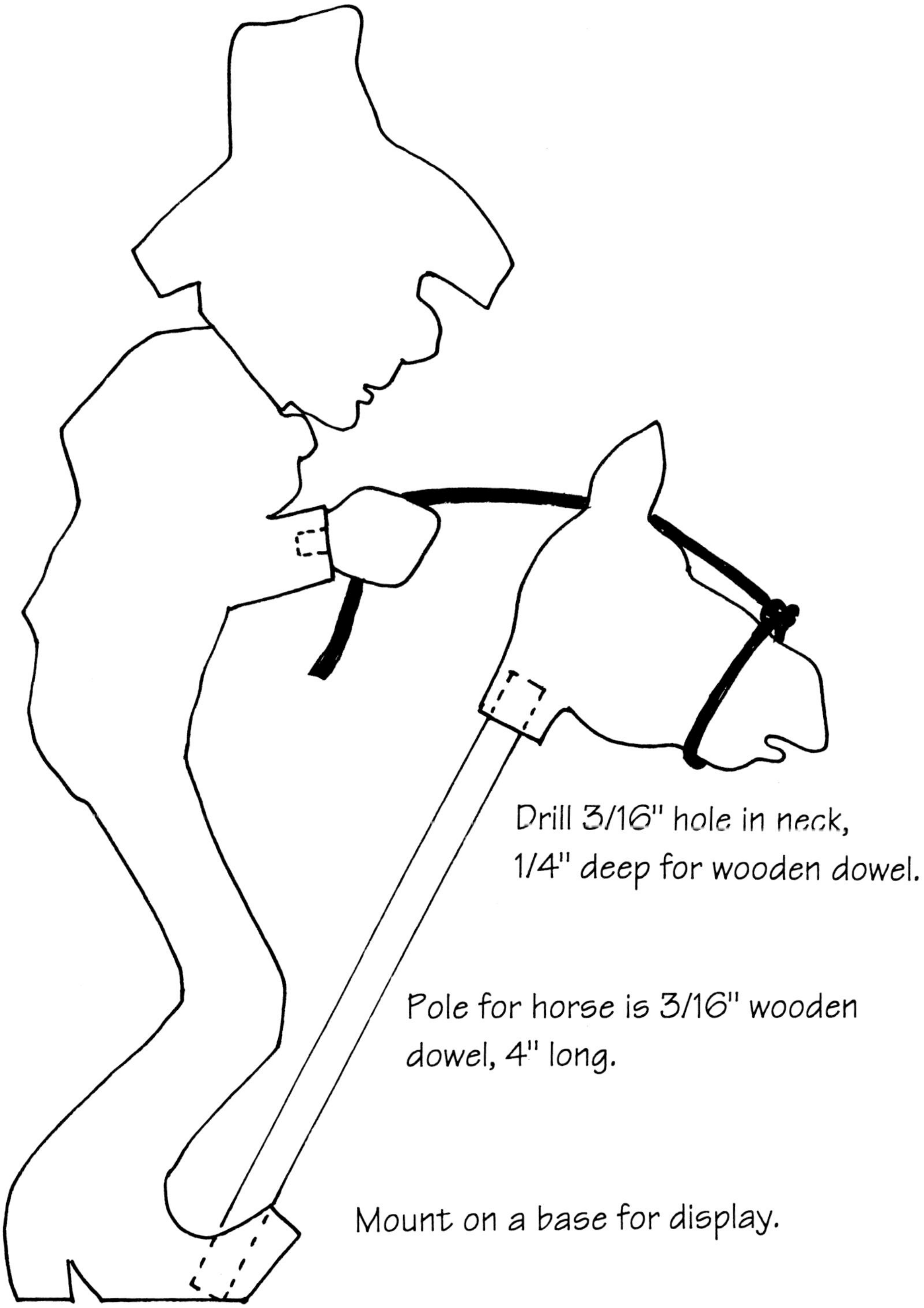

Trail Cook #1

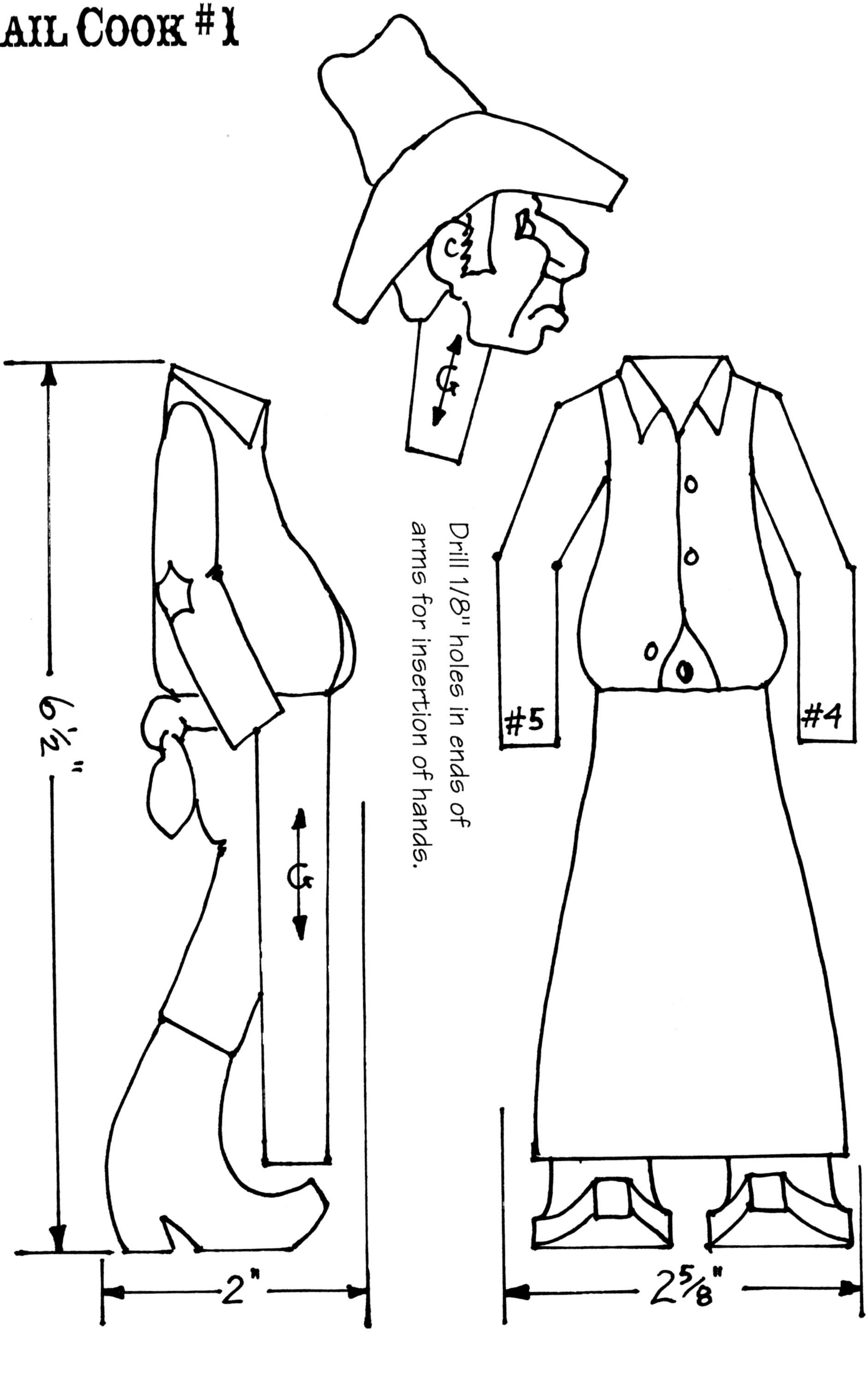
6½"
2"
2⅝"
#5
#4
Drill 1/8" holes in ends of arms for insertion of hands.

Trail Cook #2

Cookpot is a wooden candle holder cup available at craft stores, or made from scrap wood. Handle and hanger hook are made from scrap wire. Use heavy thread to hang pot from tripod.

Spoon is made from scrap wood.

Cigarette is made from a small piece of toothpick.

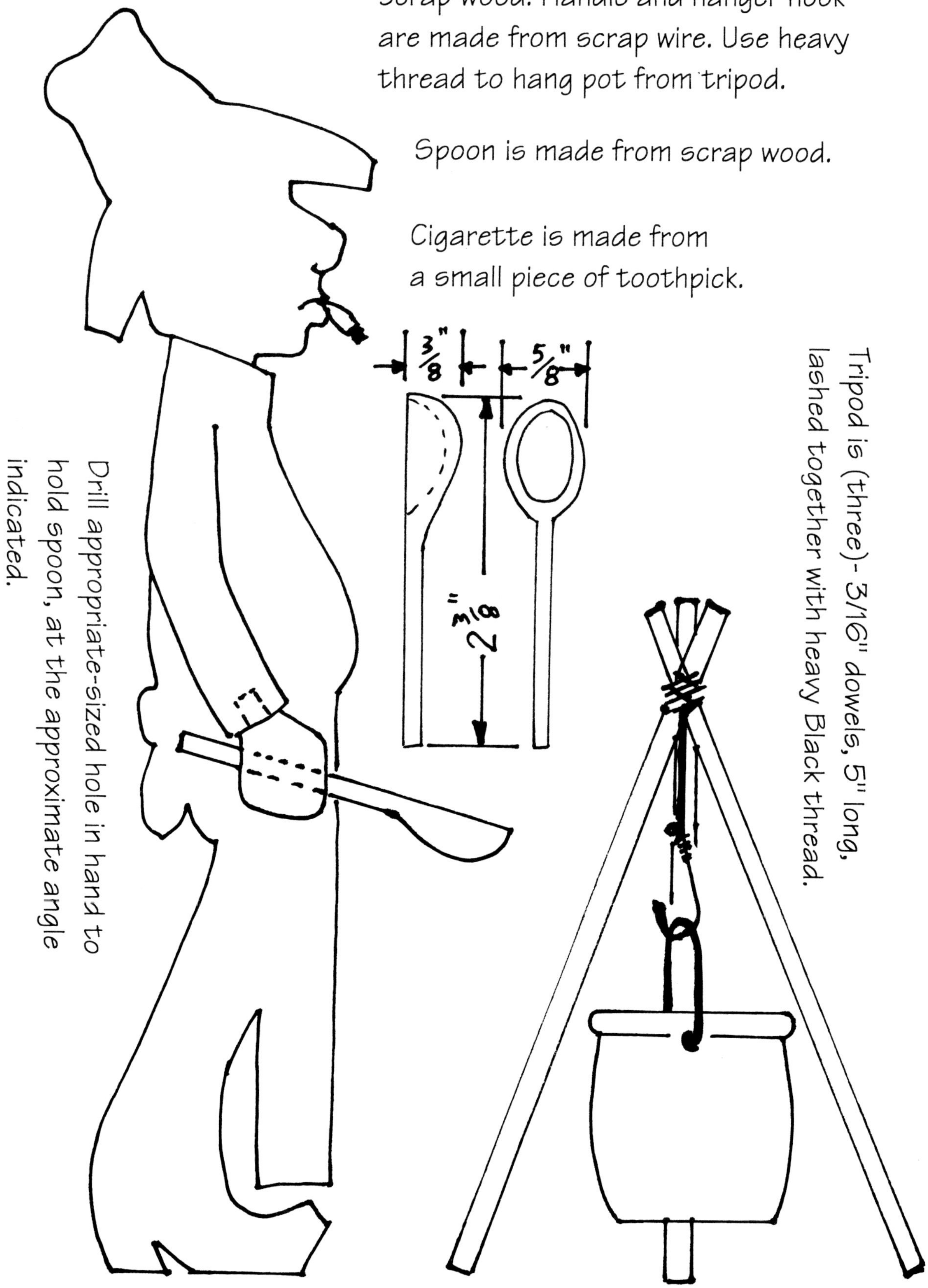

Drill appropriate-sized hole in hand to hold spoon, at the approximate angle indicated.

Tripod is (three)- 3/16" dowels, 5" long, lashed together with heavy Black thread.

Mount on a base for display.

Tough Luck #1

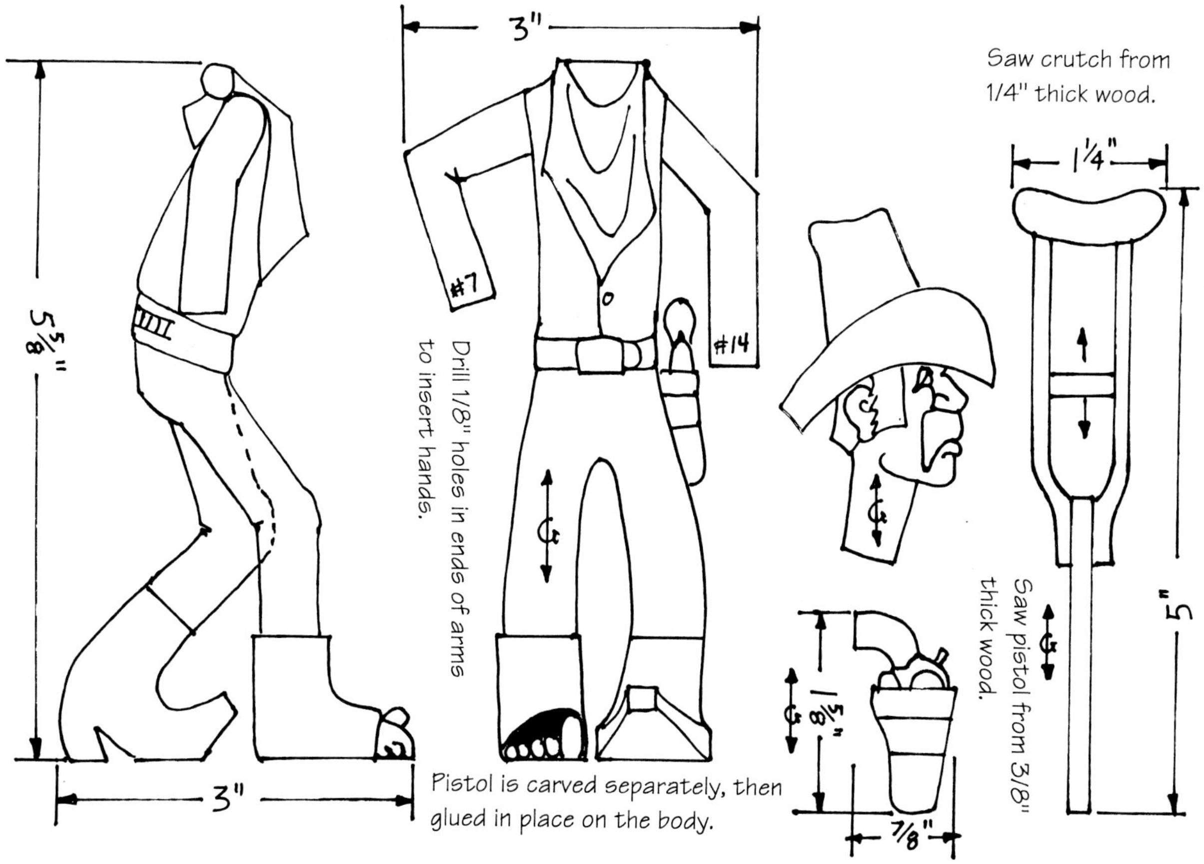

Tough Luck #2

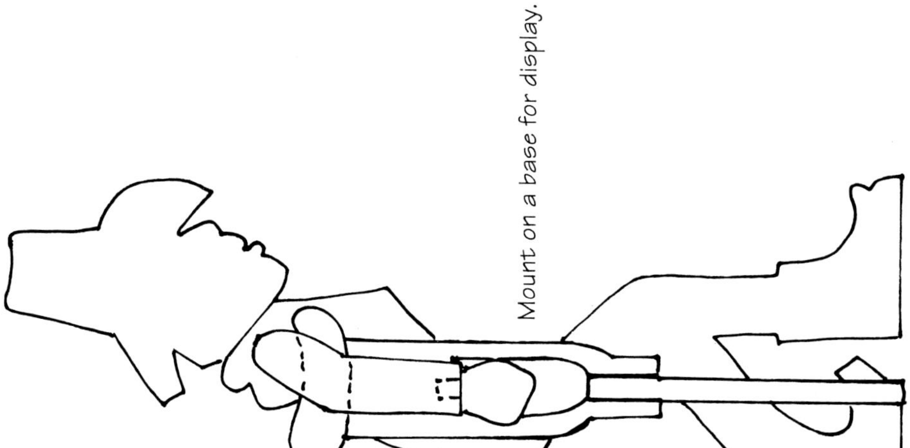

Crutch is made from scrap wood. Attach hand to right arm, then adjust hand grip on crutch so it fits in the hand and crutch pieces. When all parts fit properly, glue the hand grip in place.

Pages 16 and 17 must be enlarged 135% for original size.

Help Me Turn Him Loose: #1

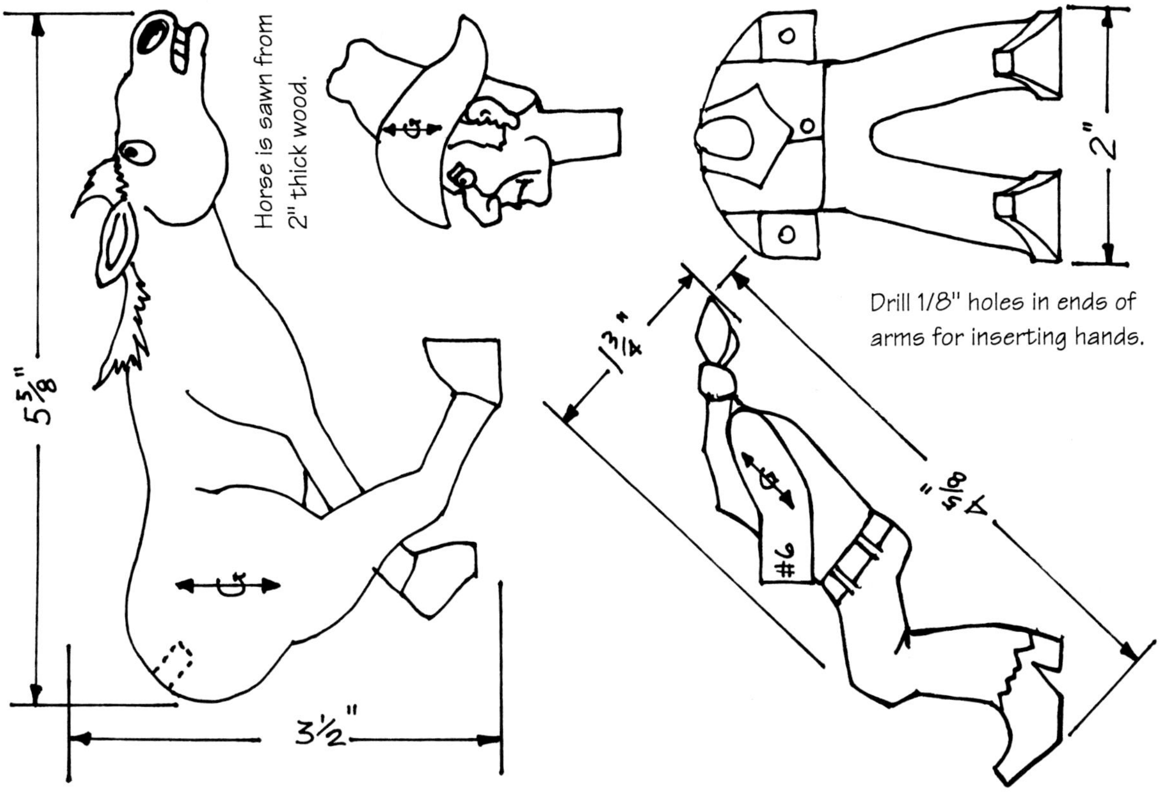

Help Me Turn Him Loose: #1

Drill a 1/8" hole in rear of horse as indicated. Insert a tail made from unraveled rope or twine, and glue it in place.
Refer to the TIPS section for details on making realistic rope. Loop the rope around the nose of the horse ,and run it through 1/8" holes drilled through the hands.

If desired, refer to the TIPS section for details about making barbed-wire, and add it as indicated on the pattern.

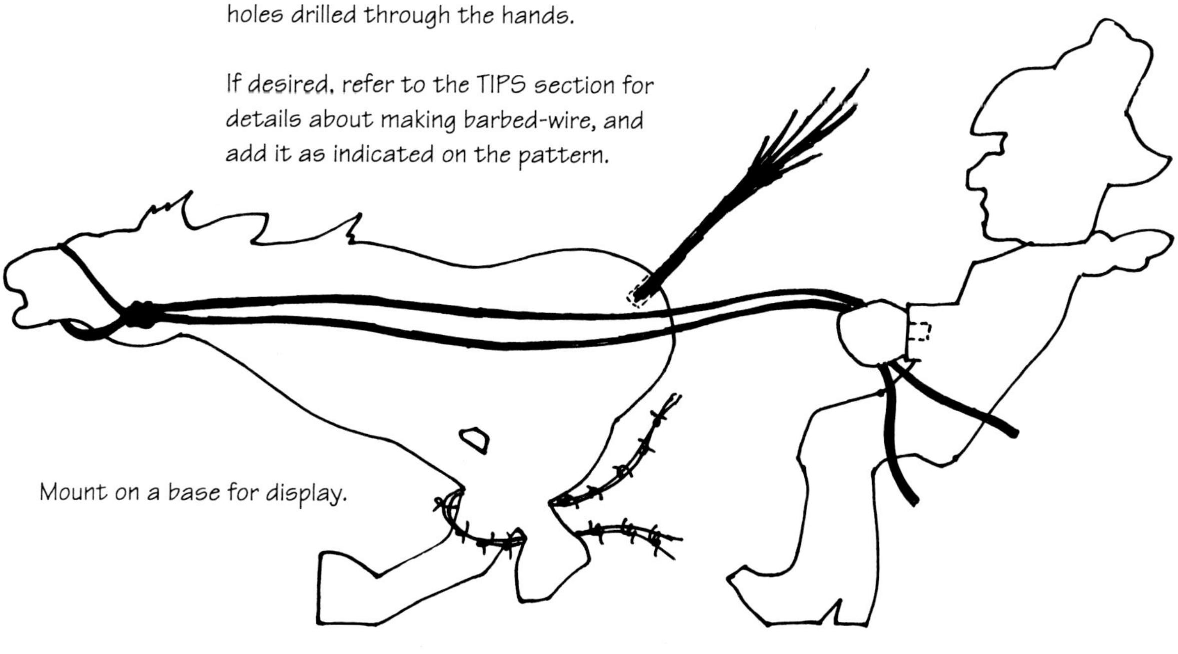

Mount on a base for display.

I NEED A CAREER CHANGE #1

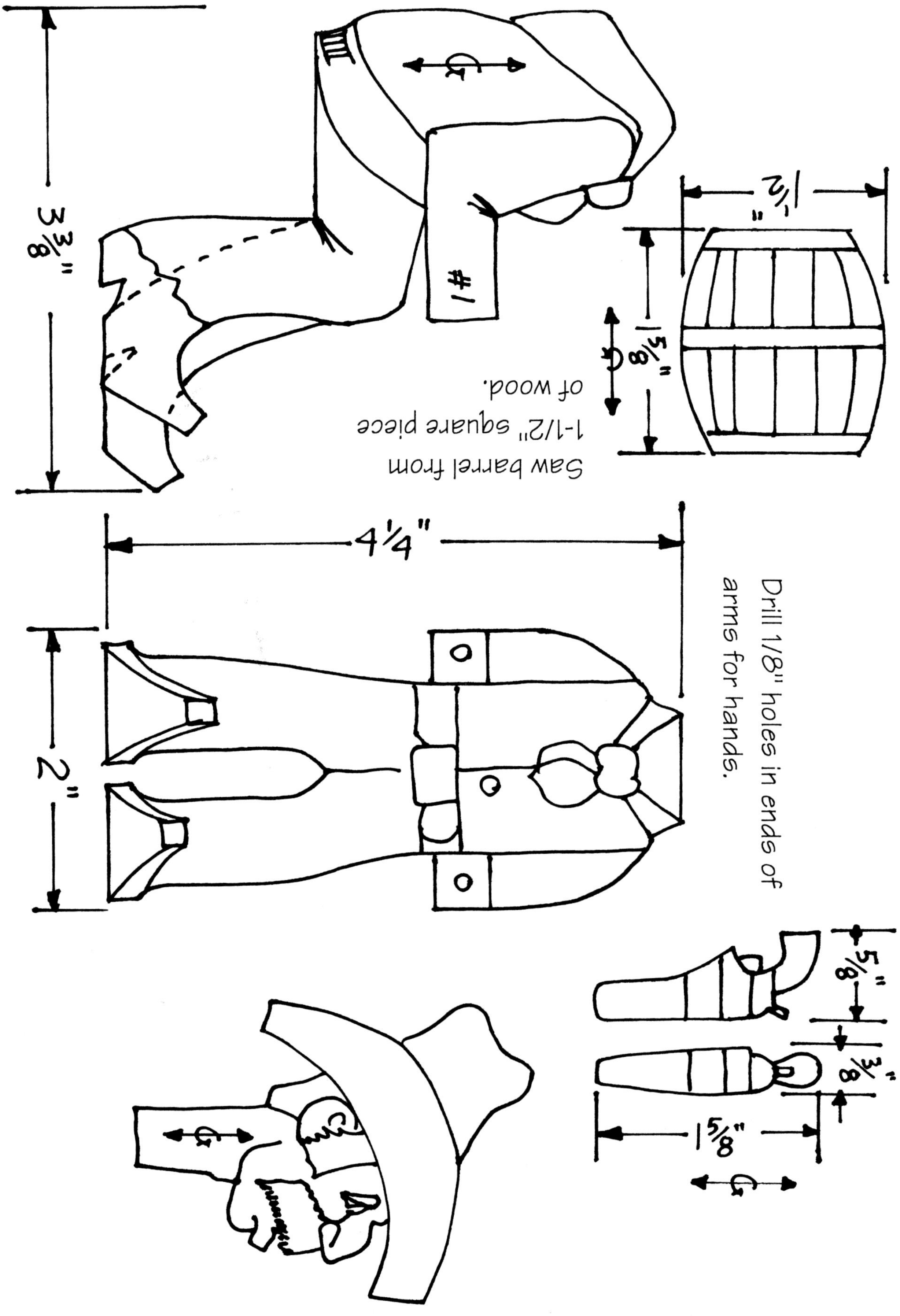

I NEED A CAREER CHANGE #2

Refer to the TIPS section for details on making realistic rope.

Cigarette (optional) is made from a piece of toothpick or scrap wood.

After carving barrel and cowboy, adjust barrel height so cowboy sits flat on it.

Carve pistol separately, then glue in place after painting.

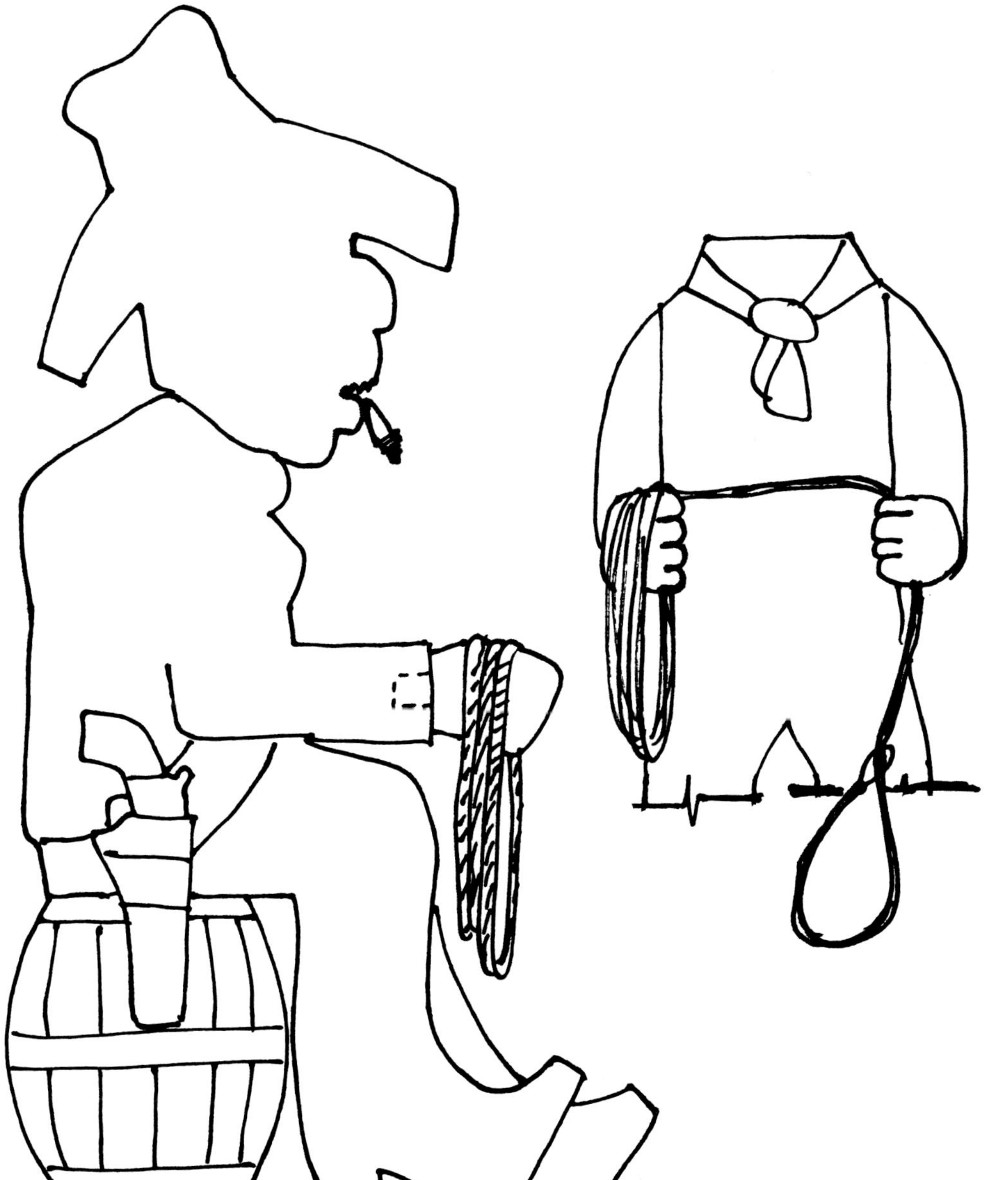

Mount on a base for display.

Indians–Run! #1

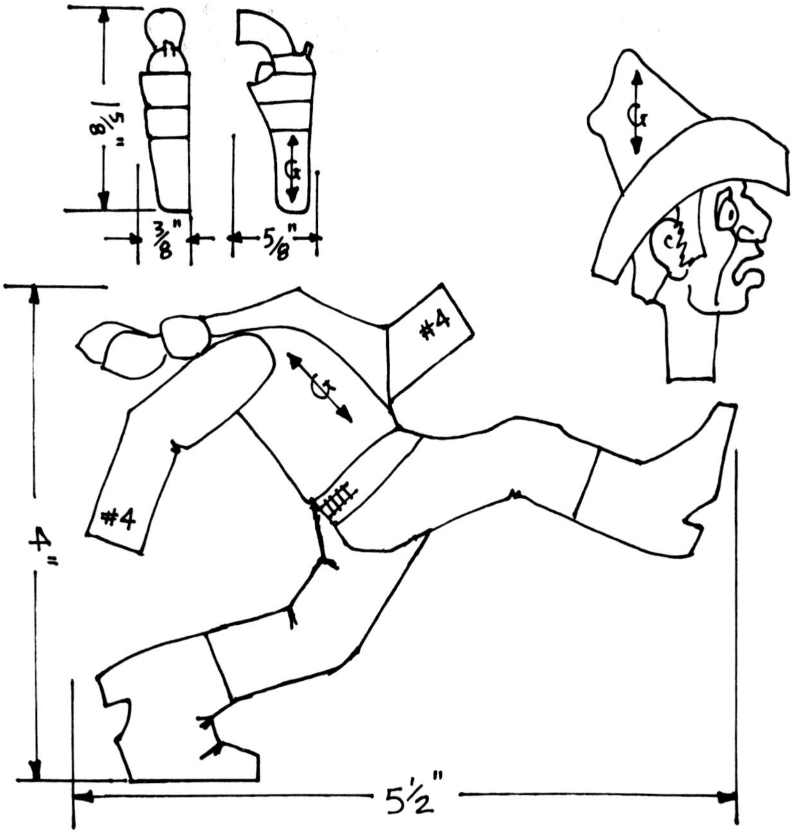

Drill 1/8" holes in ends of arms for hands.

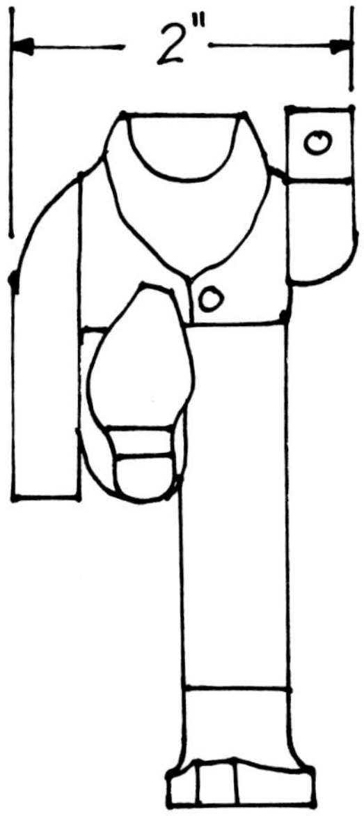

Indians–Run! #2

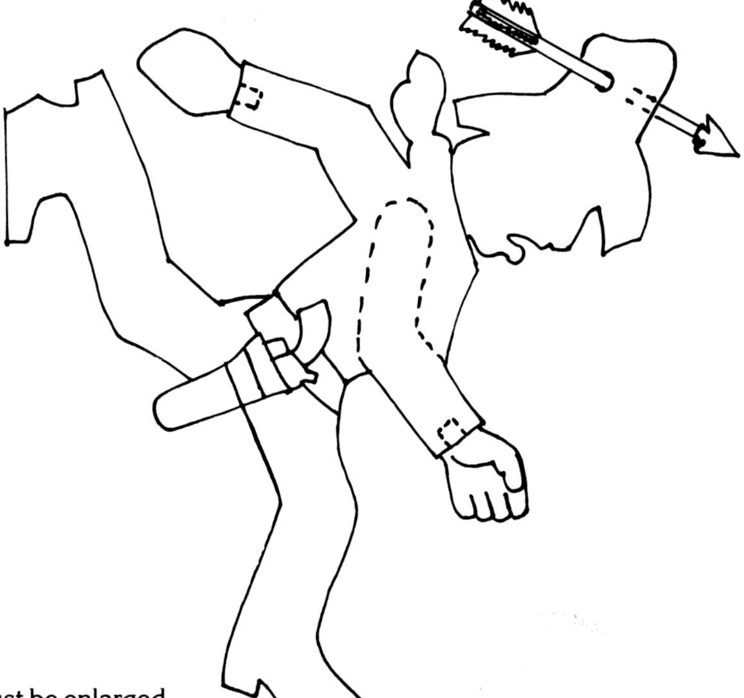

Arrow is made from scrap wood. Drill a small hole through the hat crown. Cut the arrow in half, then glue one half in each hole so the arrow appears to be going through the hat. Additional arrows may be added as desired, in locations of your choice.

Carve the pistol separately, then glue it in place after painting.

Mount on a base for display.

This page must be enlarged 135% for original size.

Wild Night— Rough Morning

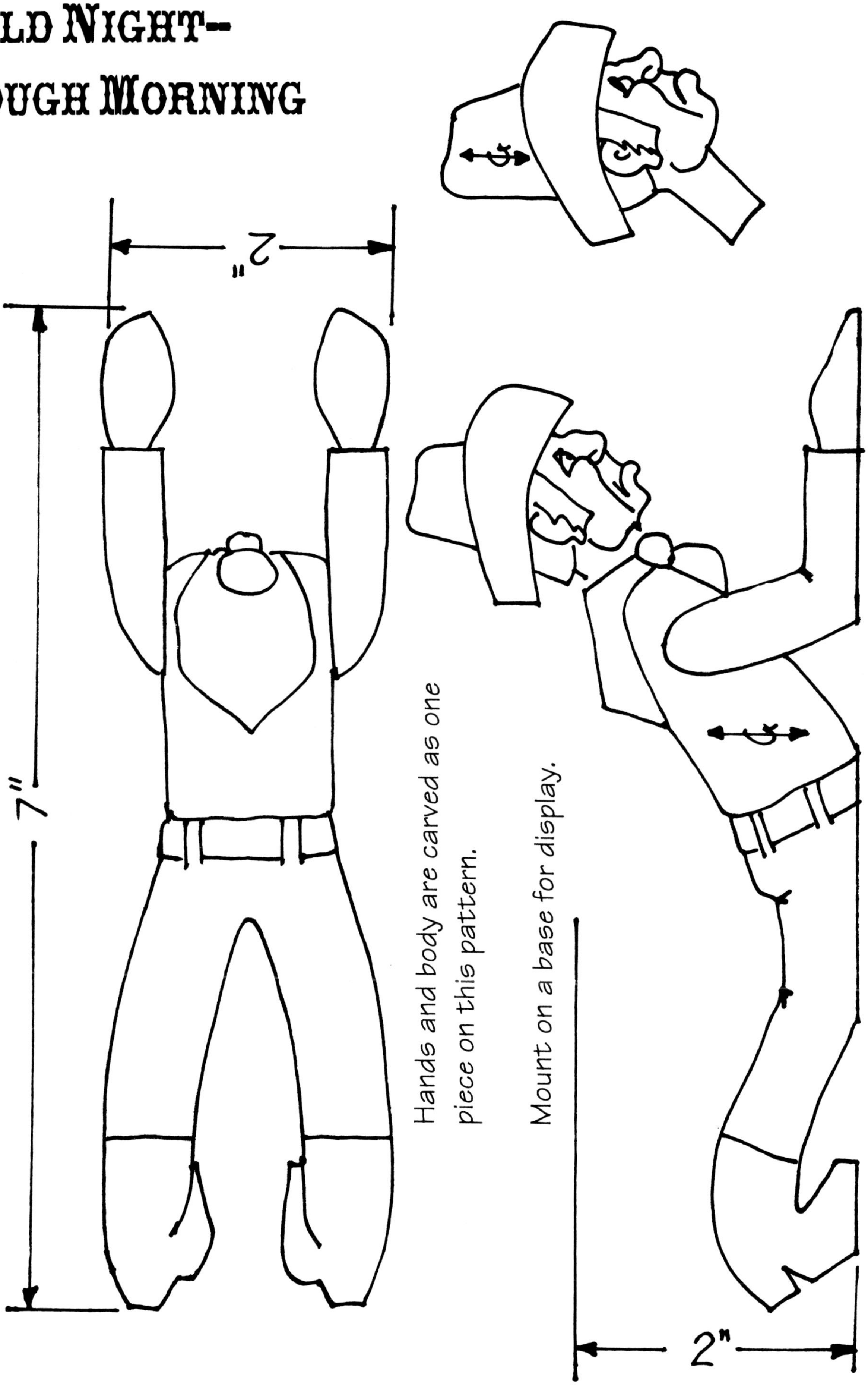

I'M GOING FISHING #1

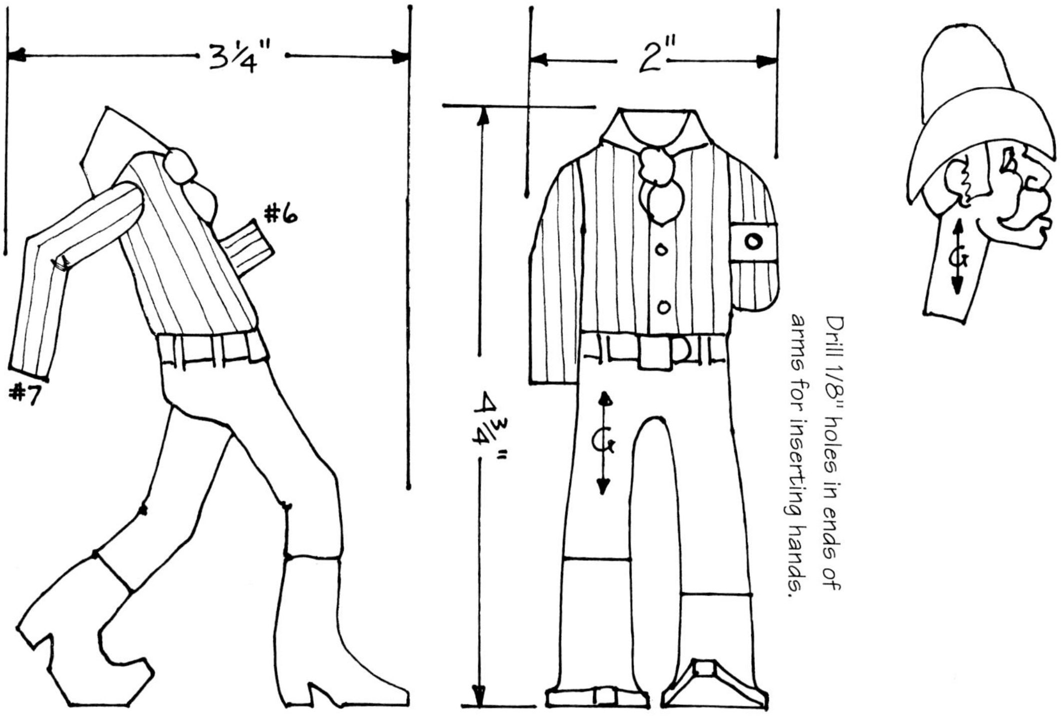

Drill 1/8" holes in ends of arms for inserting hands.

I'M GOING FISHING #2

Fishing pole is made from a section of 1/8" diameter wooden dowel, 5-3/8" in length. Use heavy Black thread for fishing line. Bobber is made from an unpainted wooden bead, available from most craft and hobby stores. A tiny peg made from scrap wood or a toothpick is used to hold the thread tightly inside the hole in the bobber. Paint the upper half White, and the lower half Red. Fish hook is just a slender piece of wire, bent to the appropriate shape.

Drill a 1/8" hole through the left hand so it can hold the pole. The other end of the pole rests on the cowboy's shoulder.

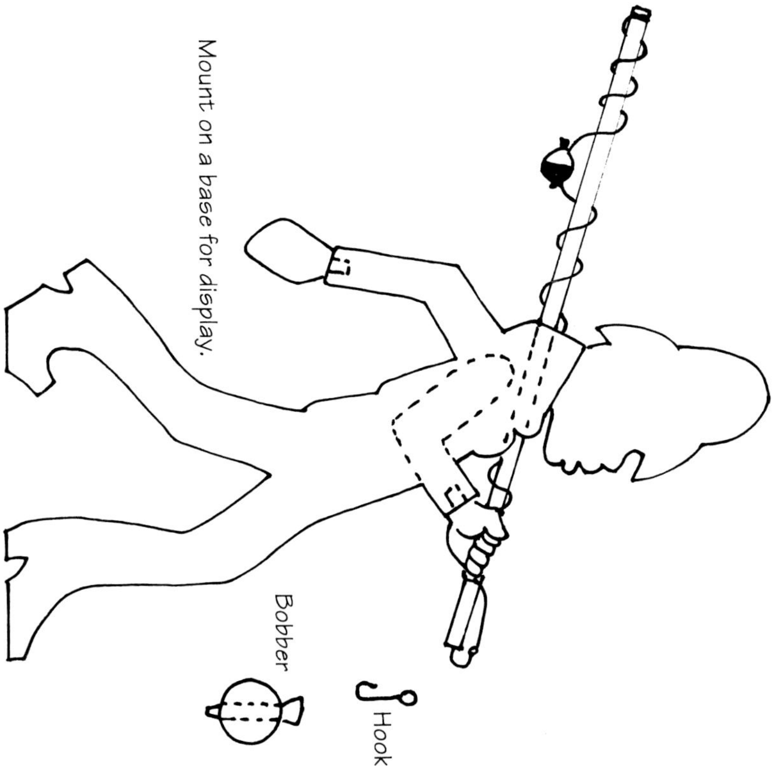

Mount on a base for display.

This page must be enlarged 135% for original size.

Who Made This Chili? #1

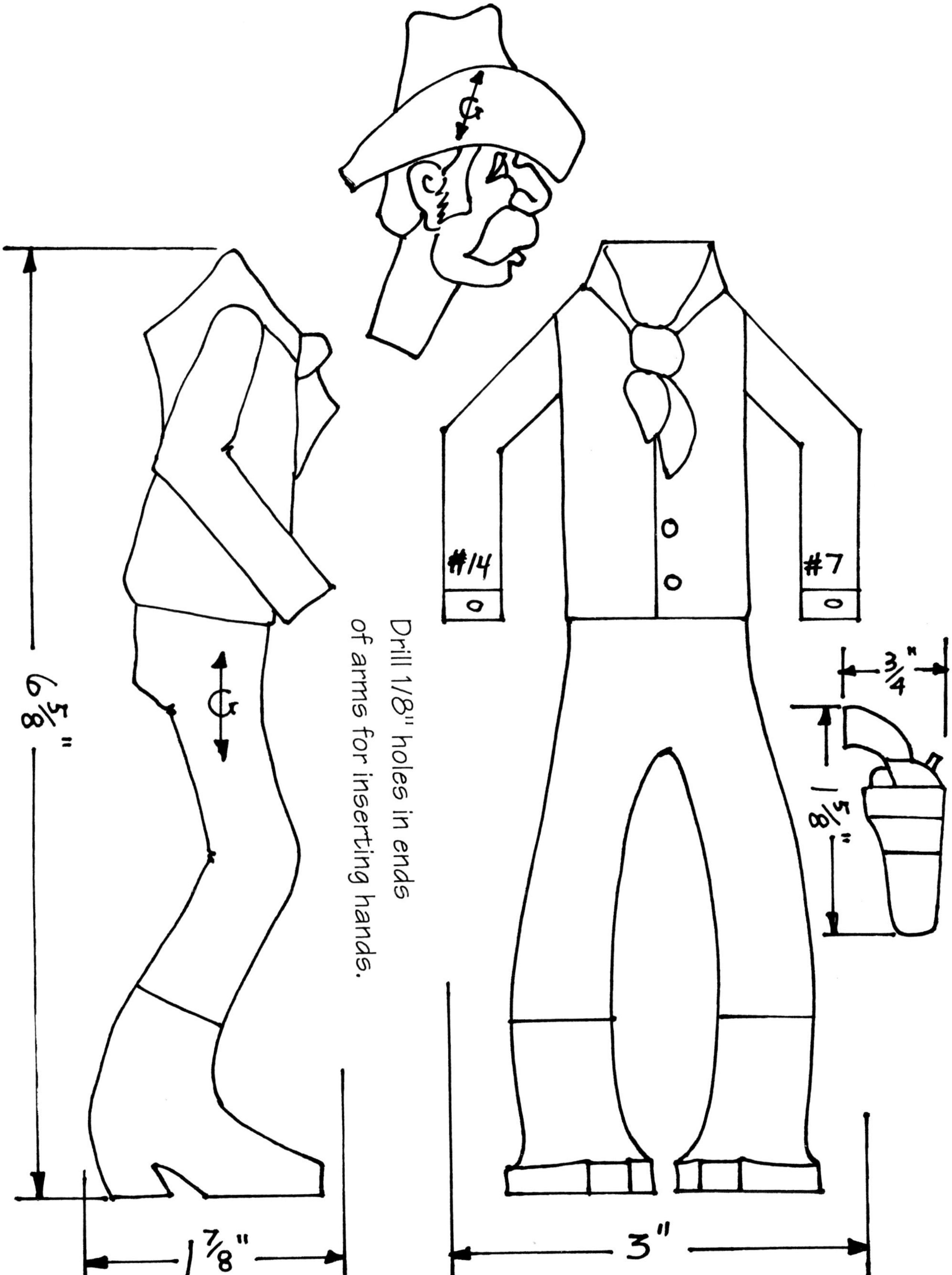

Who Made This Chili? #2

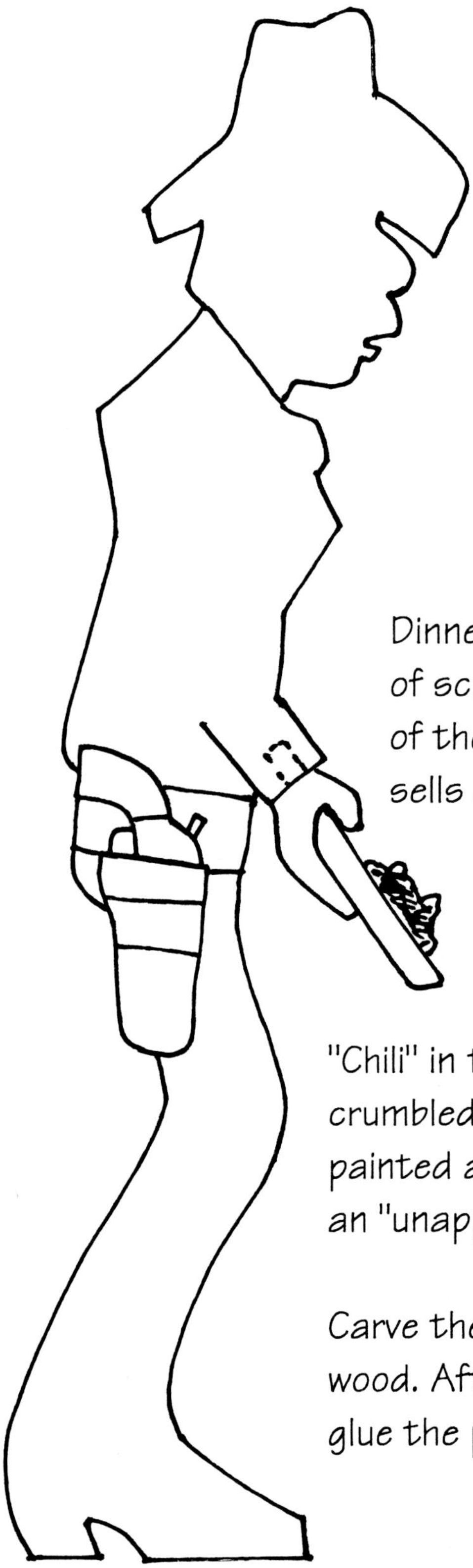

Dinner plate can be carved from a piece of scrap wood, or you may find a plate of the appropriate size in a store which sells doll and doll house supplies.

"Chili" in the plate is made from crumbled-up pieces of styrofoam, painted appropriate colors to resemble an "unappealing" meal.

Carve the pistol from 3/8" thick wood. After all painting is complete, glue the pistol in place on the gunbelt.

Cowboy With Shovel #1

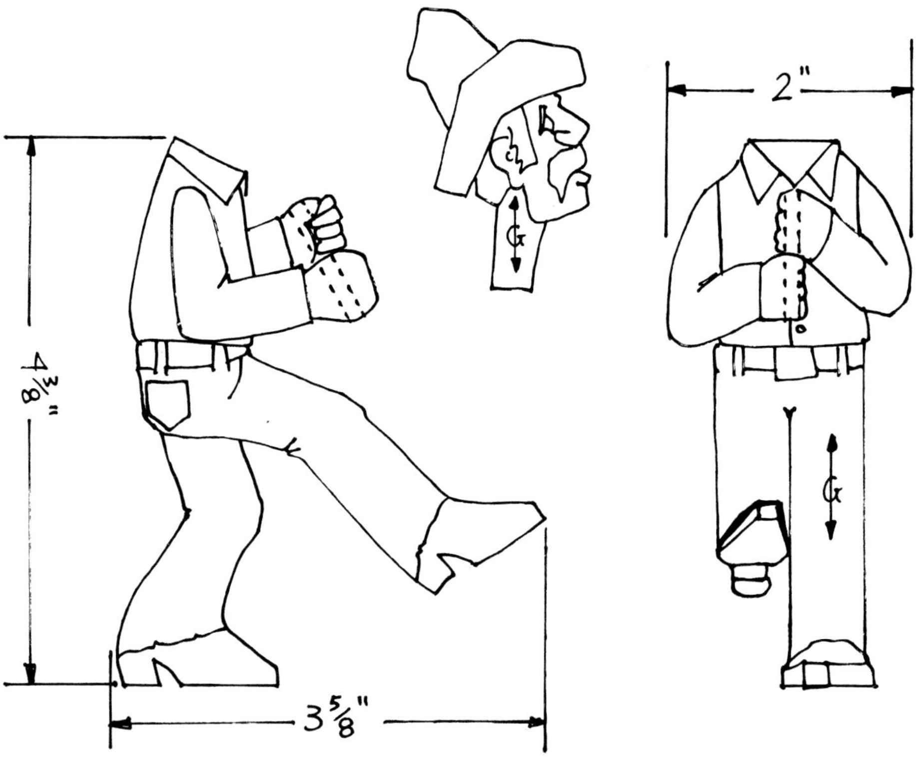

Carve the shovel first for this project. After carving the shovel, drill an appropriate sized hole through the hand section of the body, so the shovel handle will fit in the hands properly.

Cowboy With Shovel #2

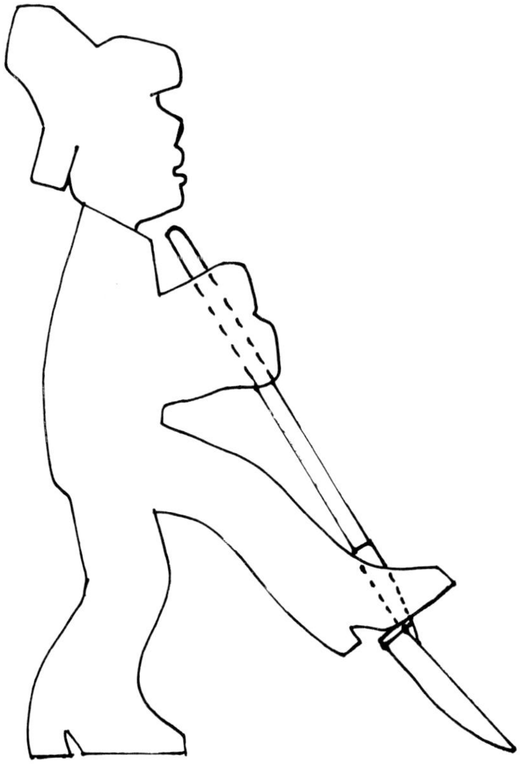

The shovel is carved from a section of scrap wood.

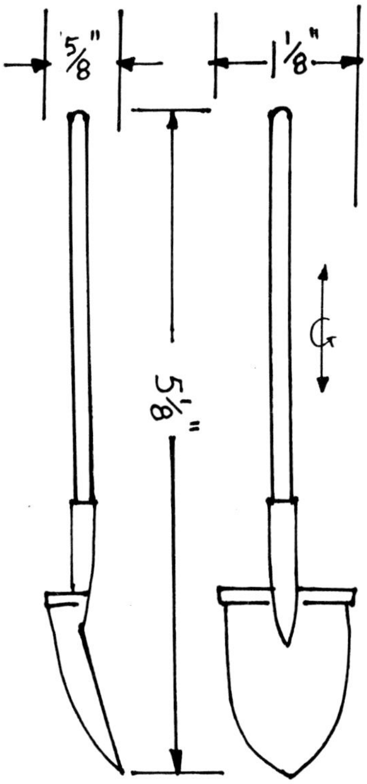

Pages 25 through 27 must be enlarged 135% for original size.

Coffee, Anyone? #1

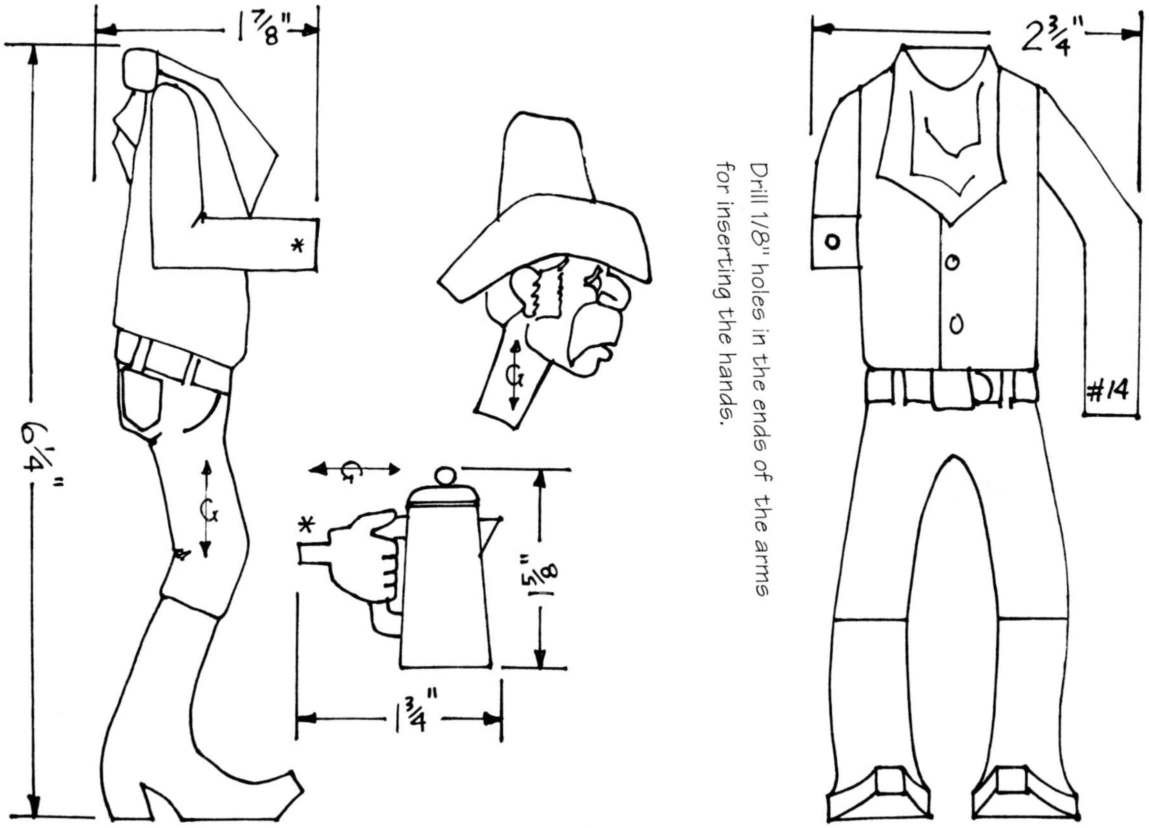

Coffee, Anyone? #2

Carve the right hand and coffee pot from a single piece of wood.

Refer to the TIPS section for instructions on painting the coffee pot to resemble that old-time speckled enamel look.

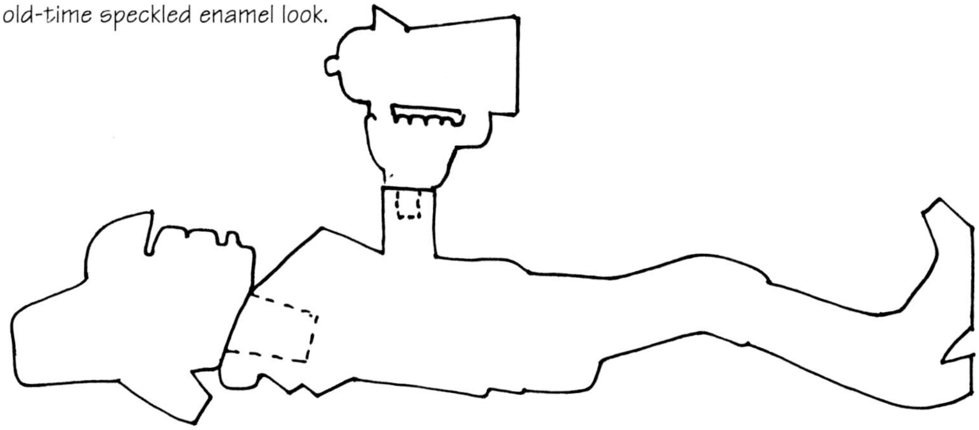

Digging Post-holes #1

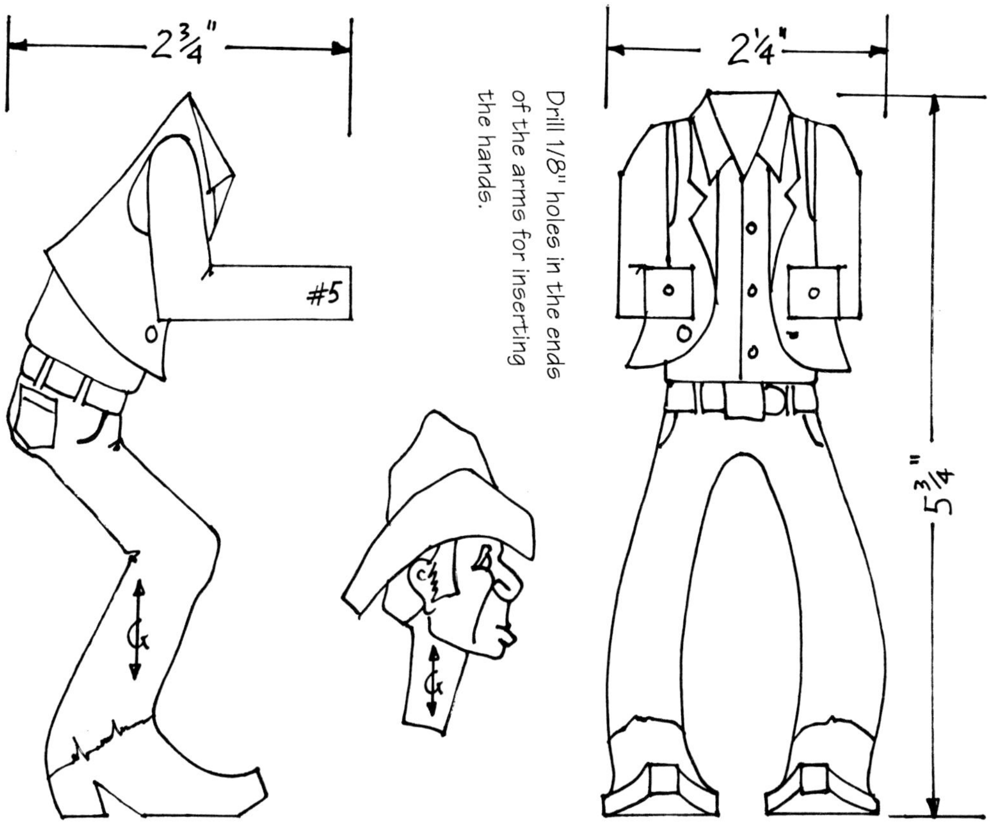

Digging Post-holes #2

Use the post-hole diggers shown here as the pattern. You may wish to carve the right and left digger pieces separately, then attach them together, or you can carve it all from one piece of wood. (Your choice).
Carve the post-hole diggers first, them drill appropriate sized holes in the hands for the digger handles.

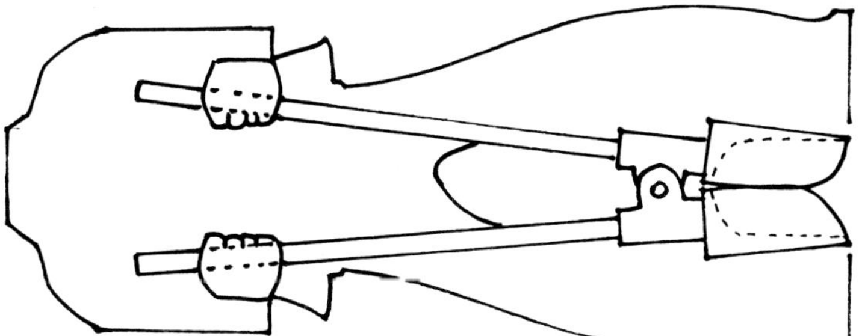

By carving the hands separately, you can position them at the proper angles to hold the digger handles.

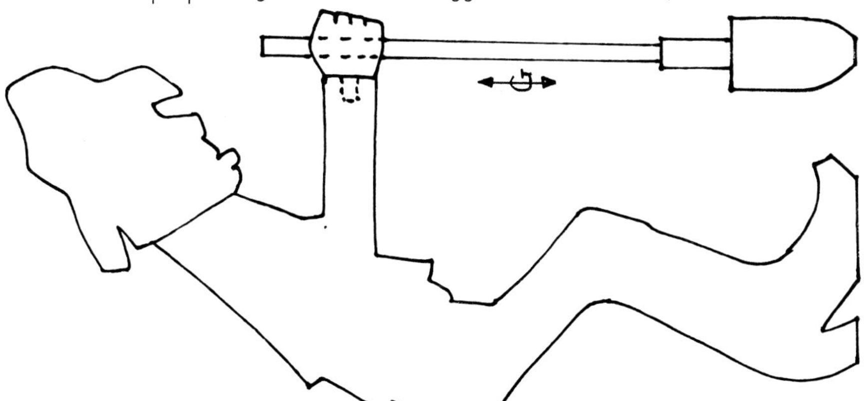

Trail Boss #1

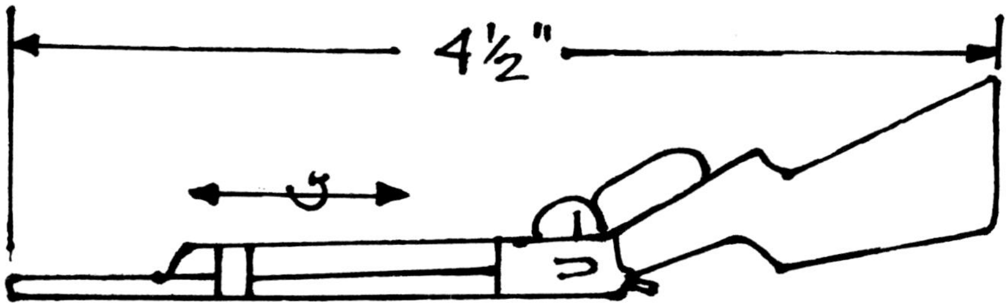

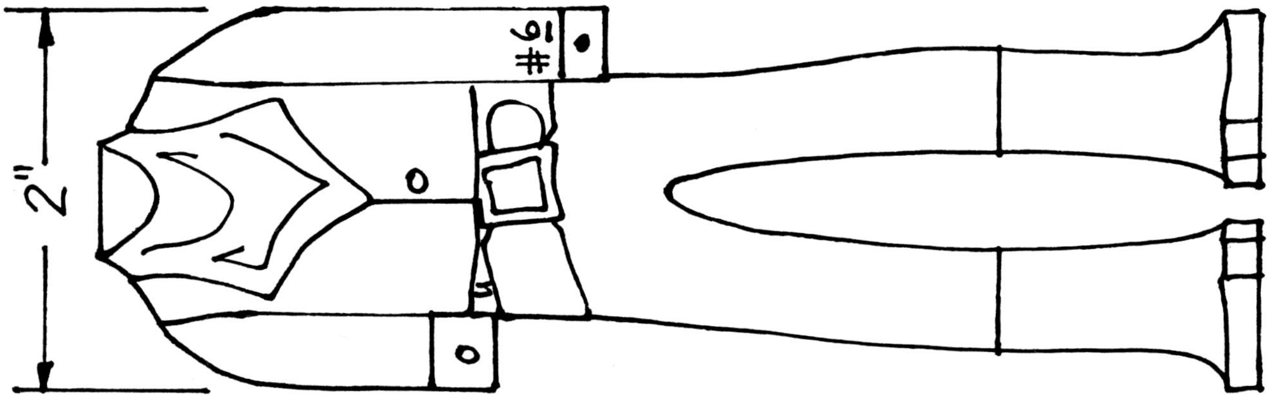

Drill 1/8" holes in the ends of the arms for inserting the hands.

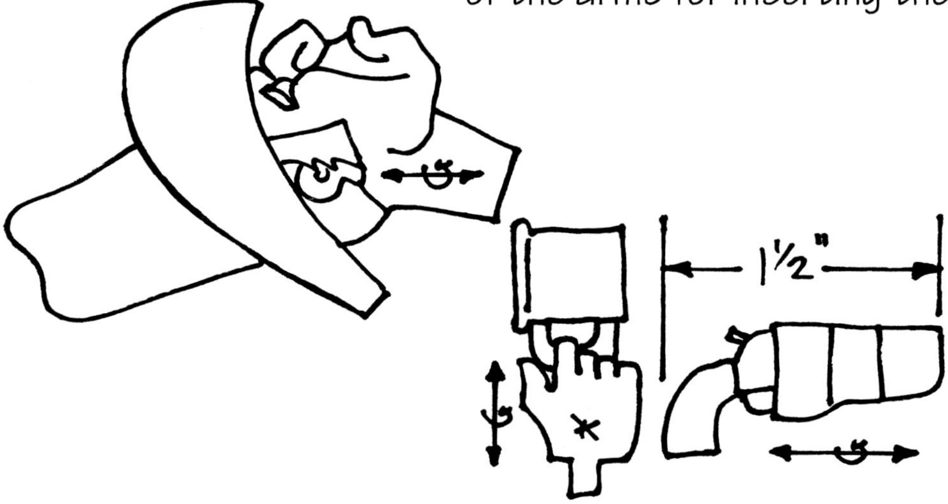

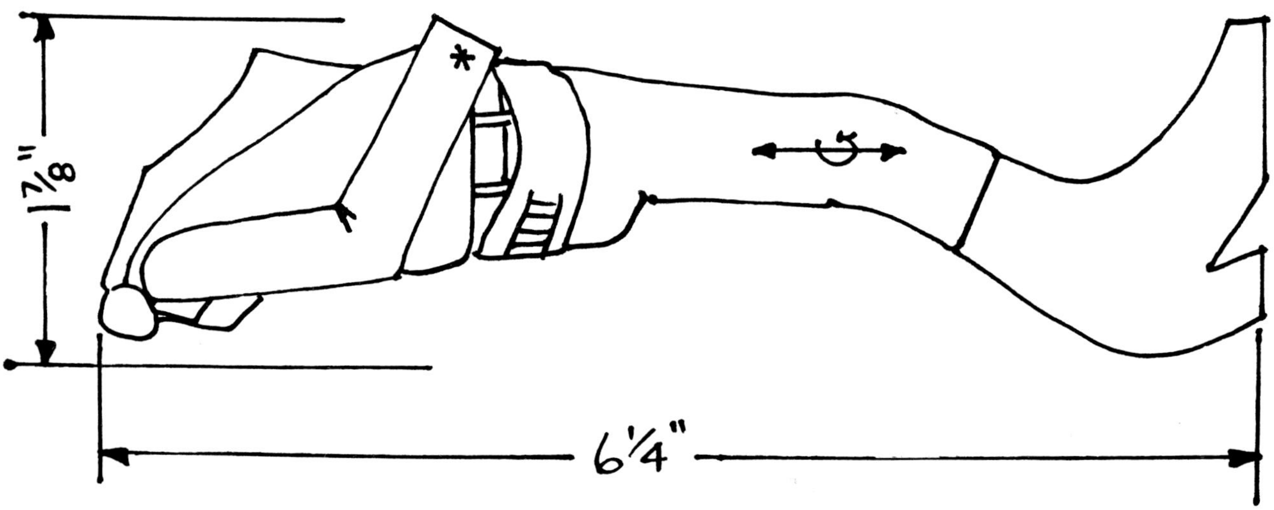

Trail Boss #2

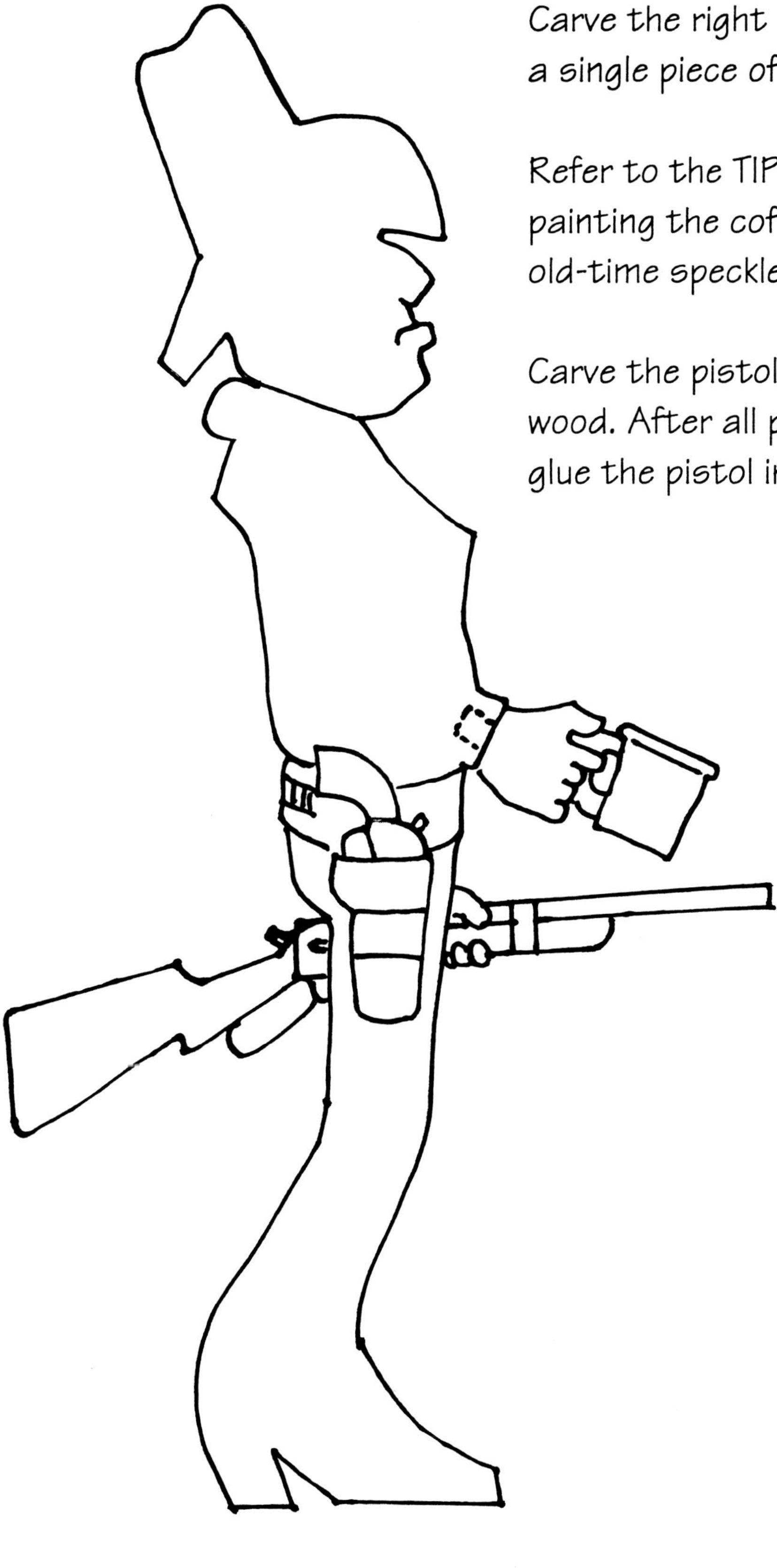

Carve the right hand and coffee cup from a single piece of wood.

Refer to the TIPS section for instructions on painting the coffee cup to give it that old-time speckled enamel look.

Carve the pistol and rifle from 3/8" thick wood. After all painting is complete, glue the pistol in place on the gunbelt.

Mending Fences #1

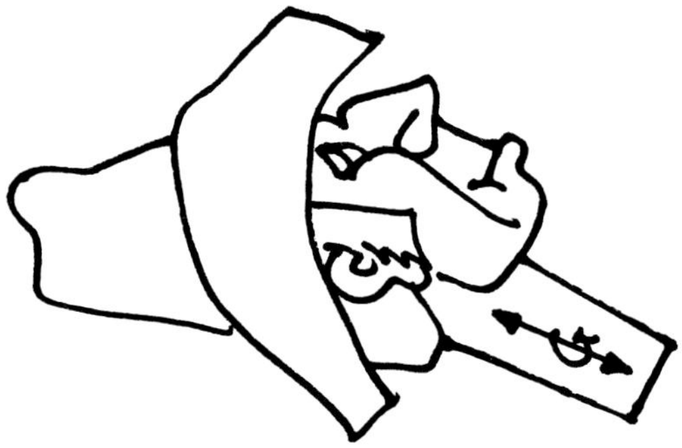

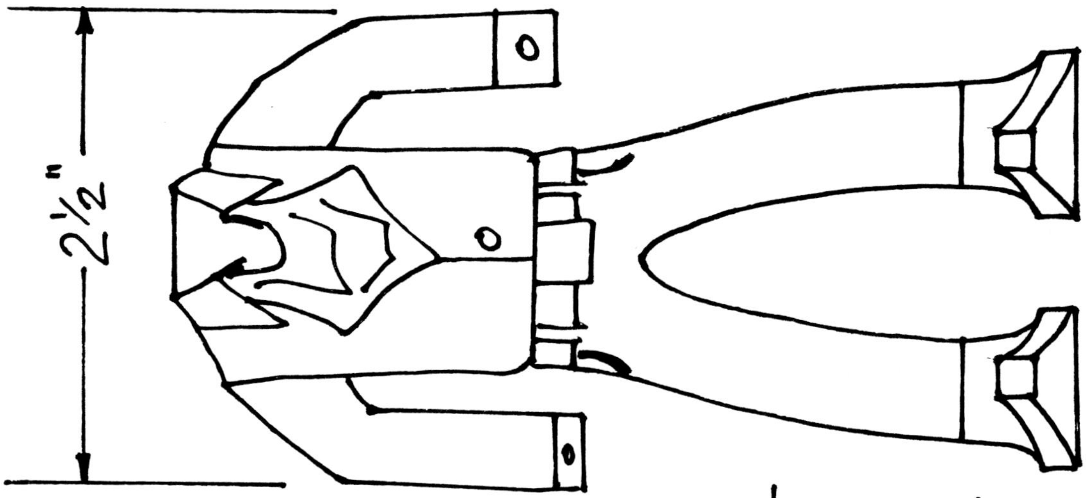

Drill 1/8" holes in ends
of arms for inserting hands.

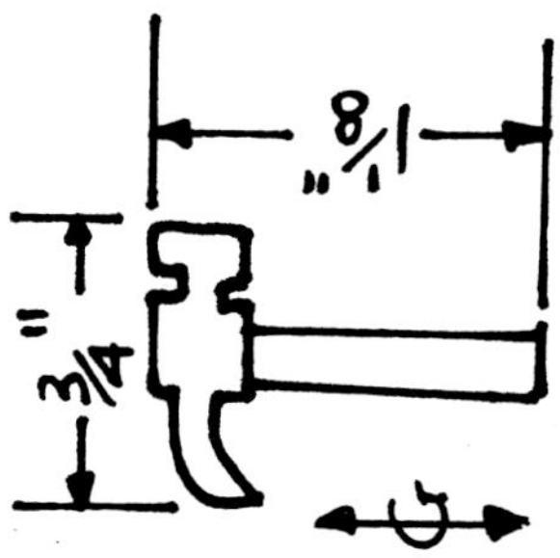

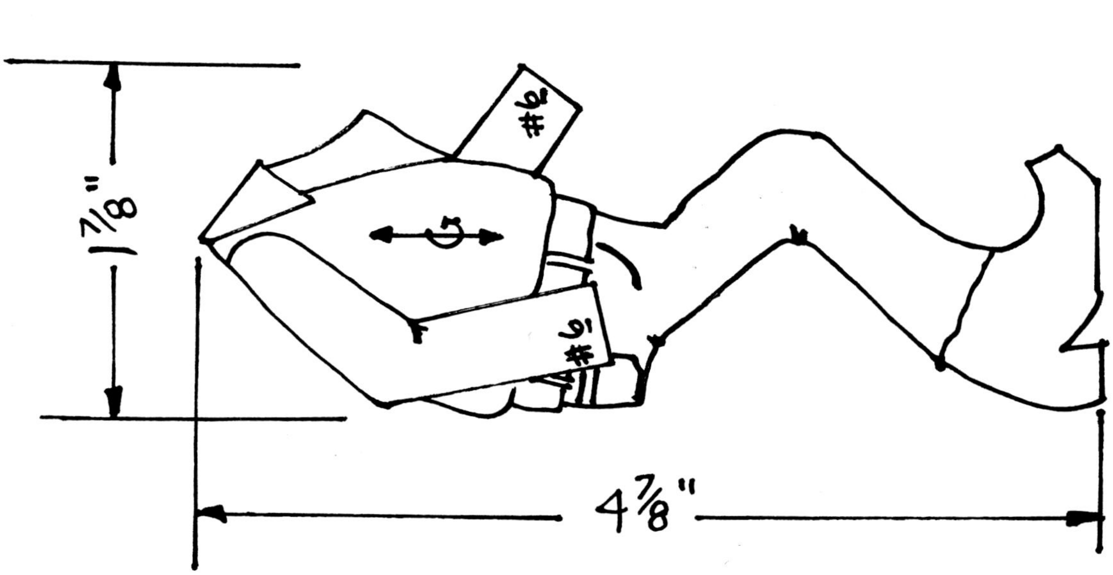

Mending Fences #2

Refer to the TIPS section for instructions on making barbed-wire, and wooden reels to wrap the wire around.

You may wish to carve this set of hands wearing gloves, since this fellow is handling barbed-wire.

The fence post is made from a small section of twig, or you can use a wooden dowel section.

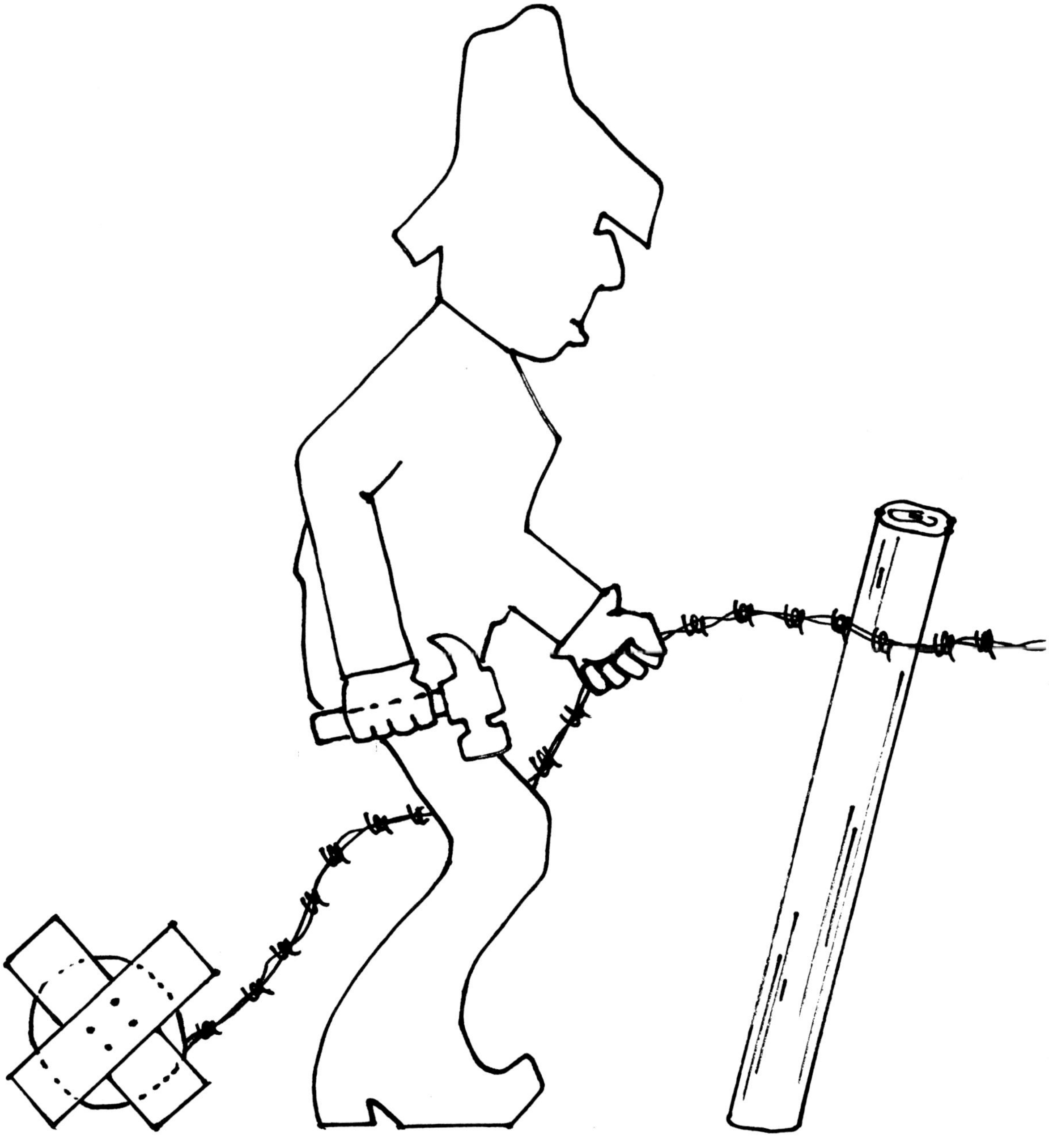

I'LL FIND WORK NEXT WEEK #1

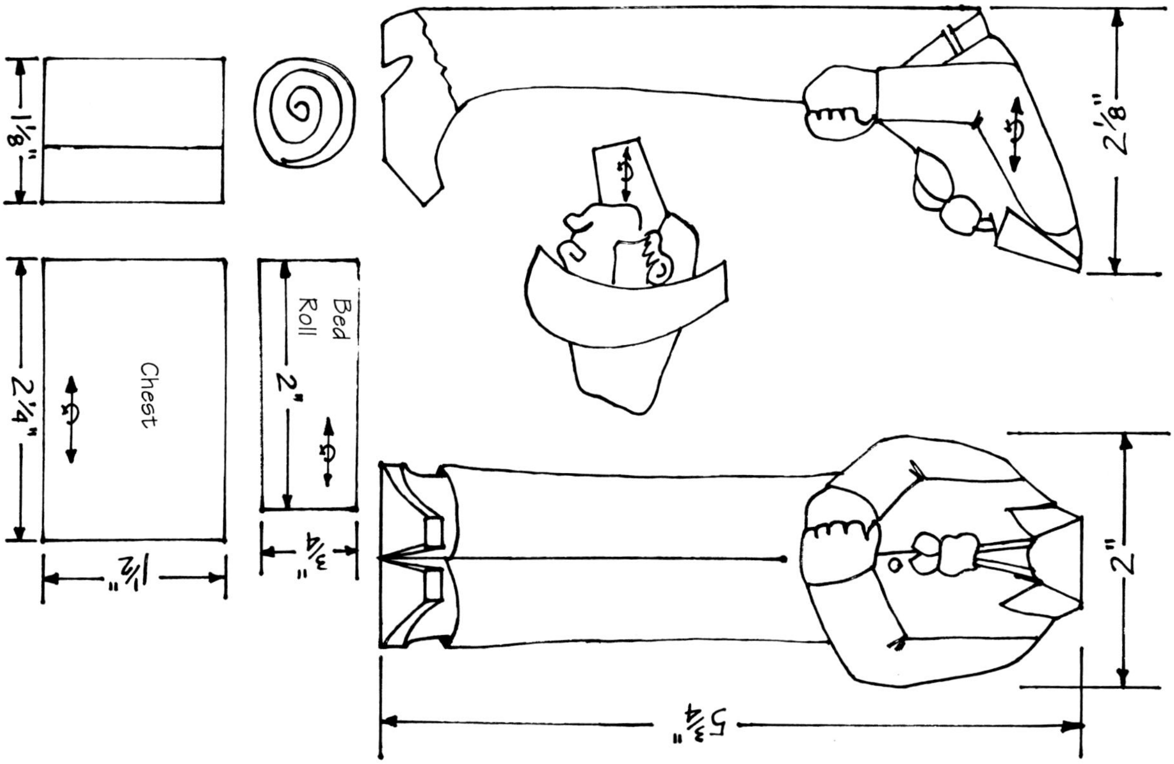

This top section must be enlarged 135% for original size.

I'LL FIND WORK NEXT WEEK #2

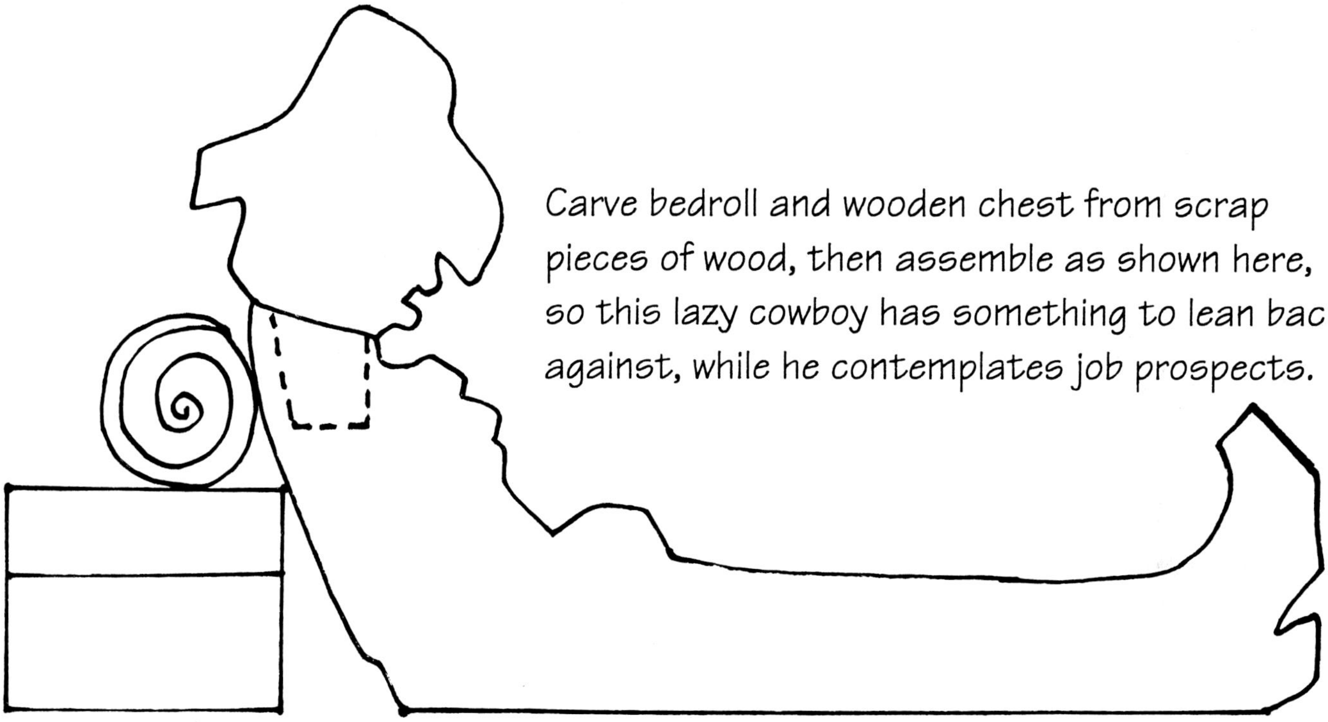

Carve bedroll and wooden chest from scrap pieces of wood, then assemble as shown here, so this lazy cowboy has something to lean back against, while he contemplates job prospects.

Gourmet Trail Cook #1

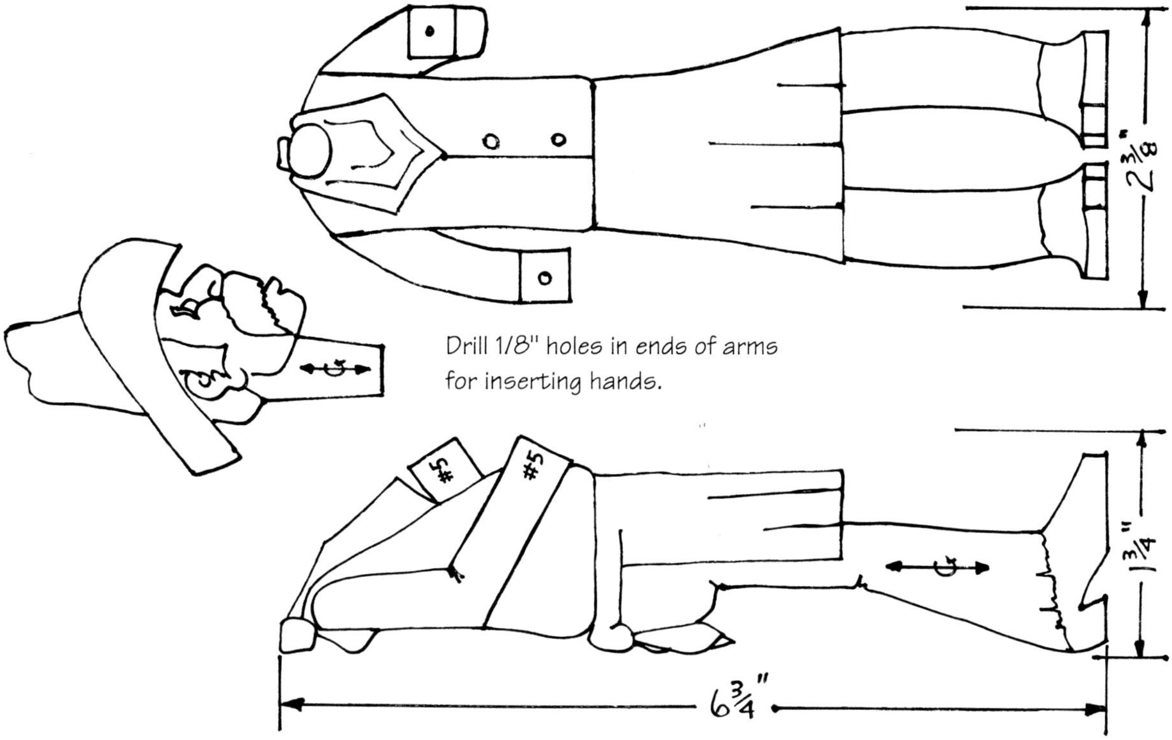

Drill 1/8" holes in ends of arms for inserting hands.

Gourmet Trail Cook #2

Carve cookpot from a piece of scrap wood. The handle is made from a section of scrap wire.
You may wish to carve a mouse with a string tail and insert it in the cook pot, to help add special "flavor" to cook's stew.

Carve the spoon from a section of scrap wood.

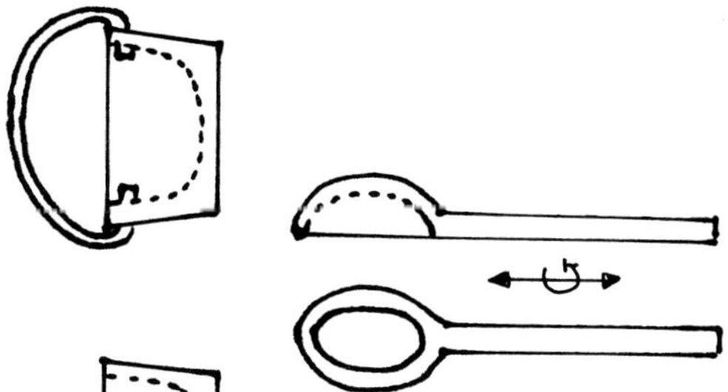

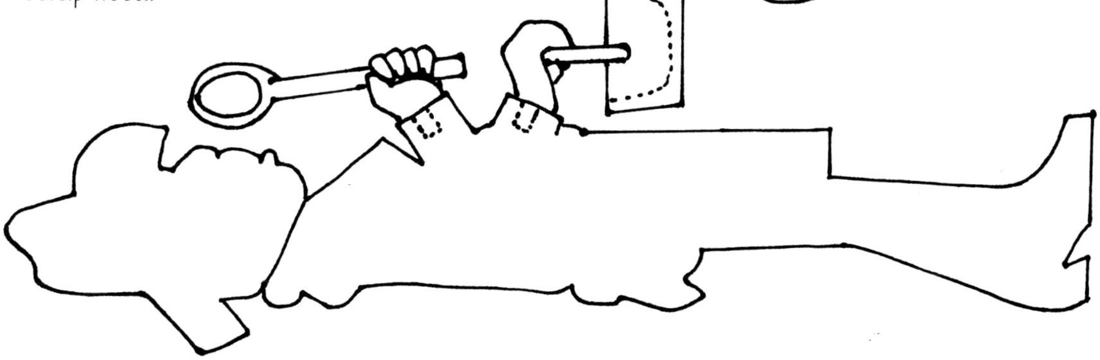

This page must be enlarged 135% for original size.

Horse Doctor #1

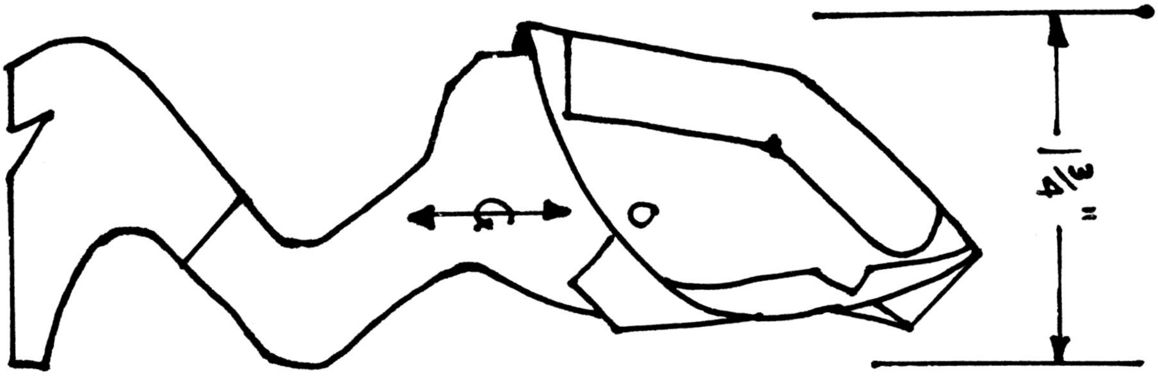

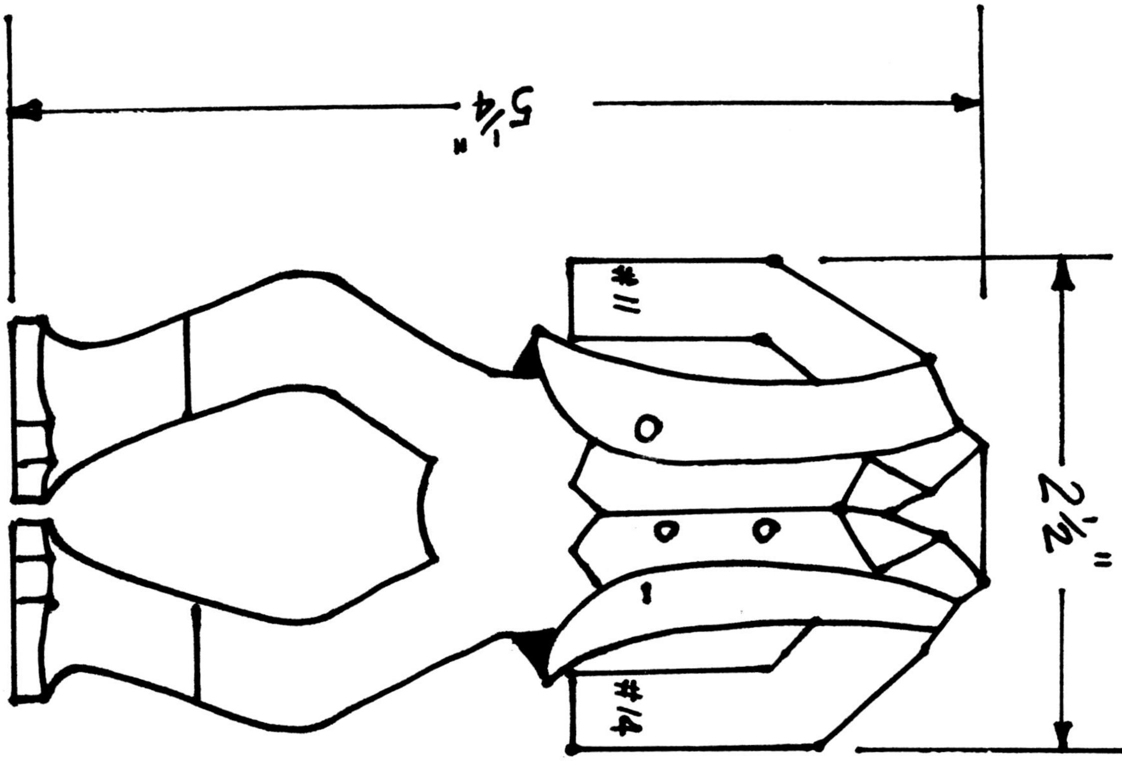

Drill 1/8" holes in ends of arms for inserting hands.

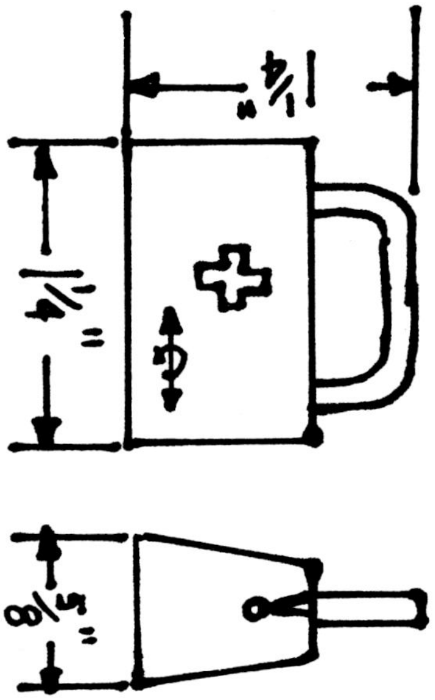

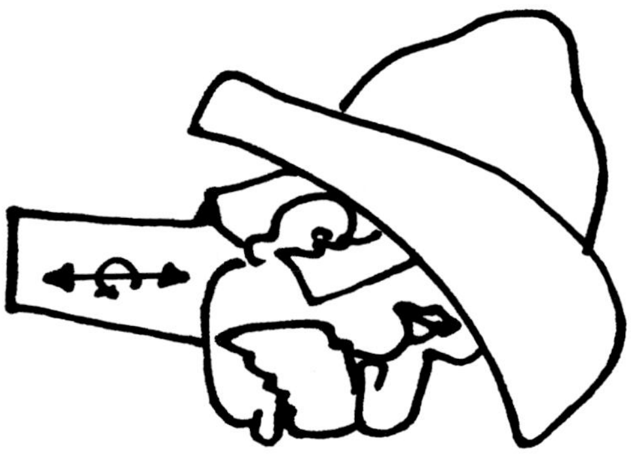

Horse Doctor #2

Carve the doctor's bag from a section of scrap wood. Make the handle for the bag from a scrap piece of wire.

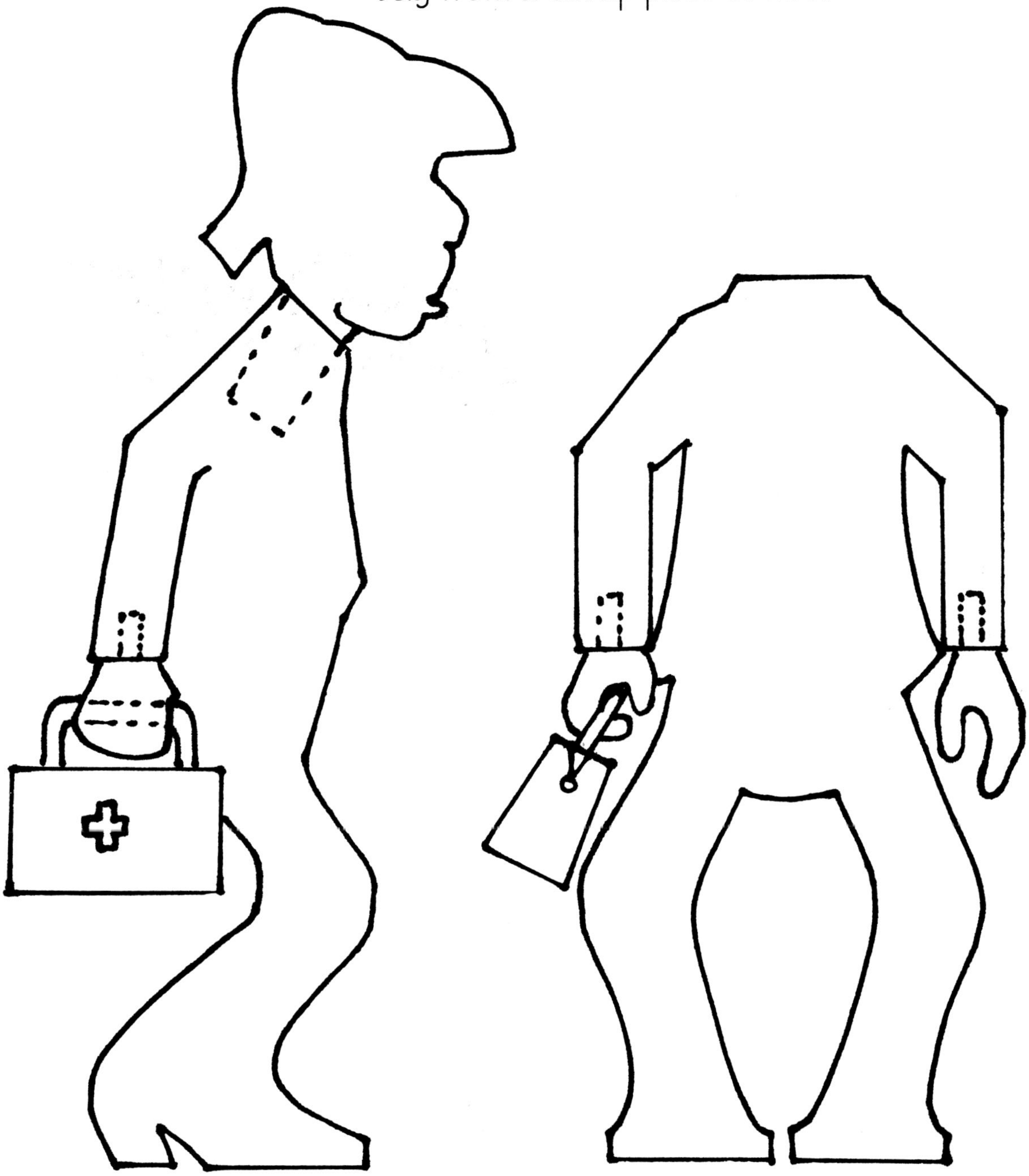

Negotiating For A Pay Raise #1

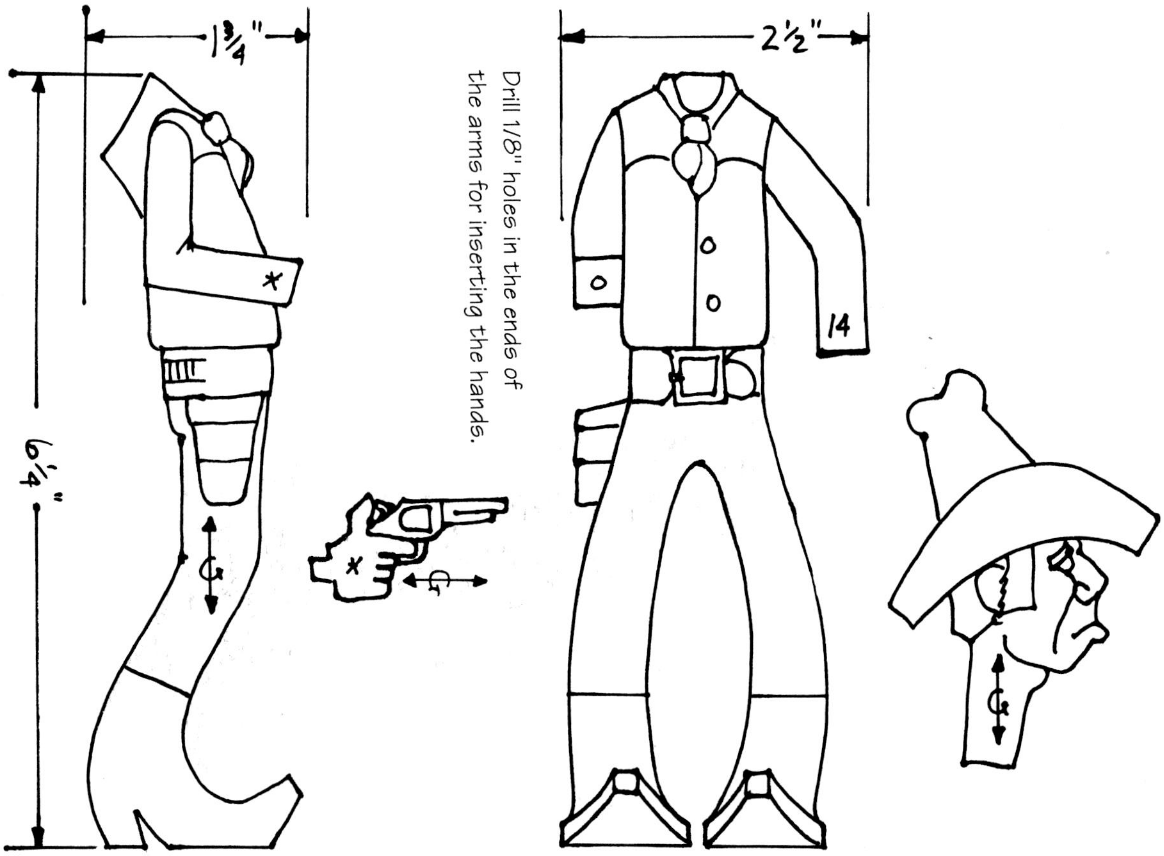

Drill 1/8" holes in the ends of the arms for inserting the hands.

Negotiating For A Pay Raise #2

Carve the right hand and pistol from a single piece of wood.

Trace the holster on the pattern, and carve it as separate piece. After all painting is complete, glue the holster in place on the gunbelt.

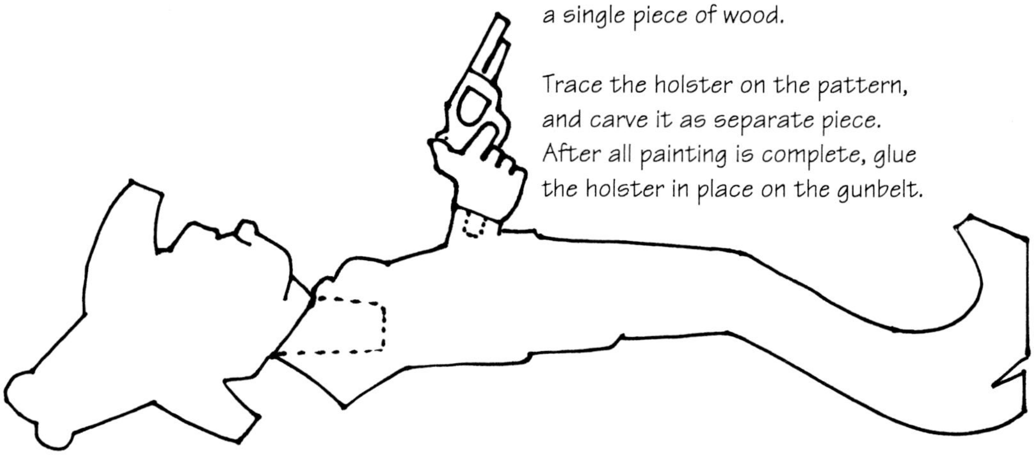

Pages 36 through 40 must be enlarged 135% for original size.

THESE BOOTS ARE TOO TIGHT!! #1

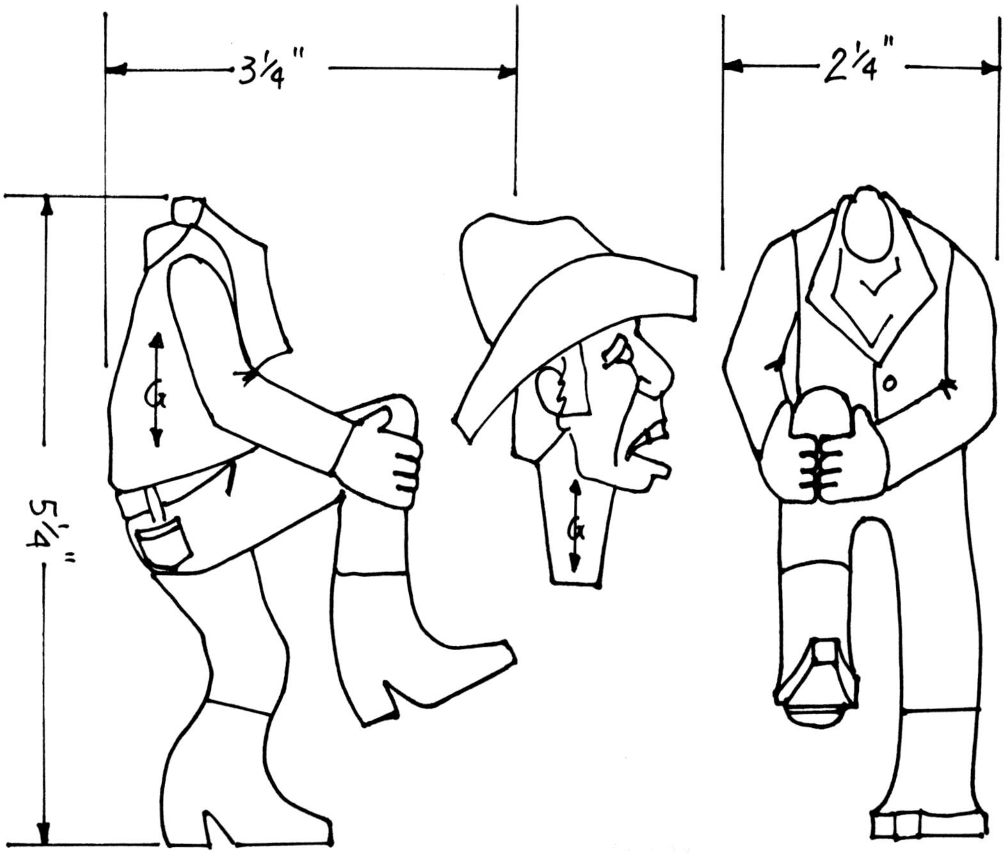

THESE BOOTS ARE TOO TIGHT!! #2

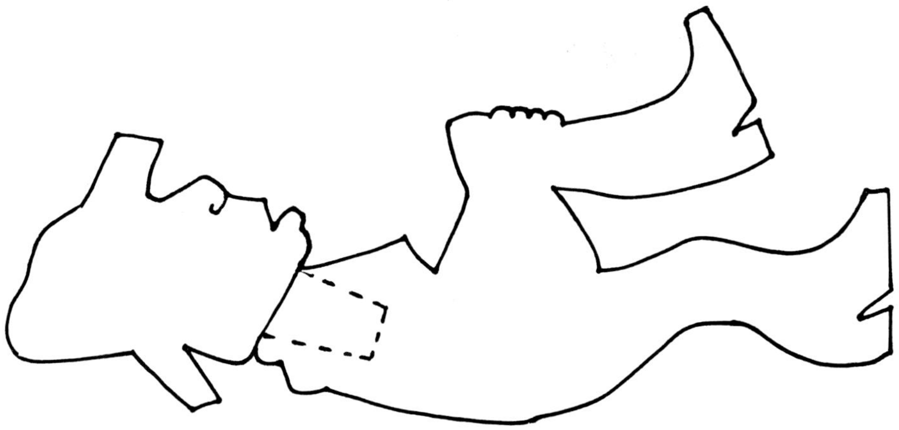

More Firewood! #1

Pay close attention to the grain direction on this one !!

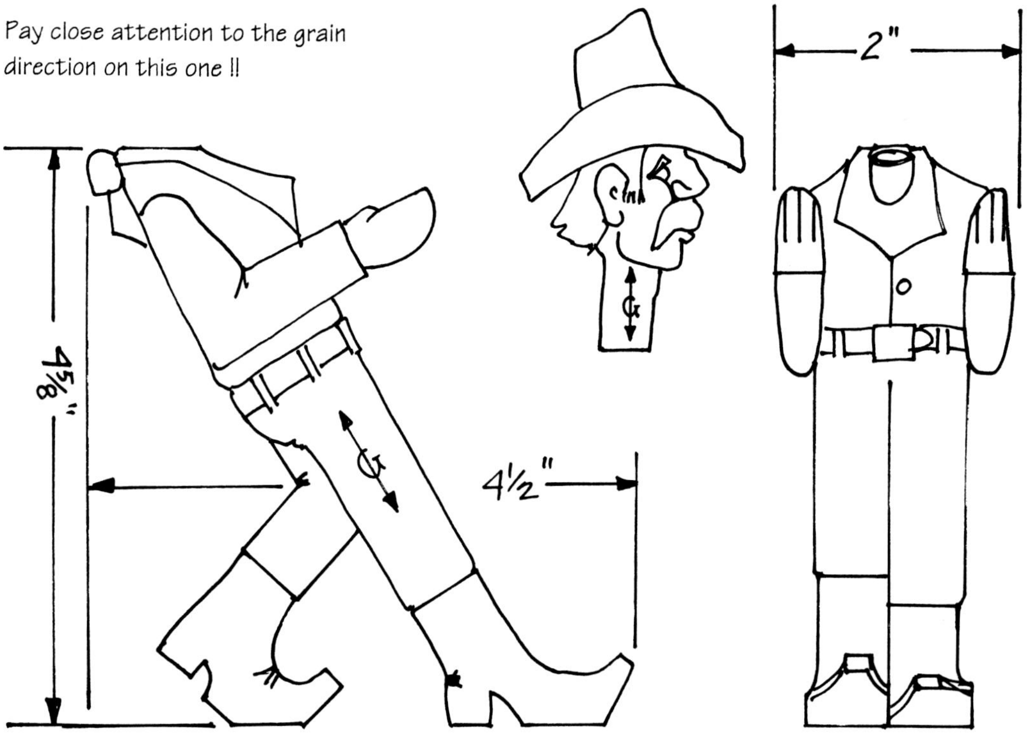

More Firewood! #2

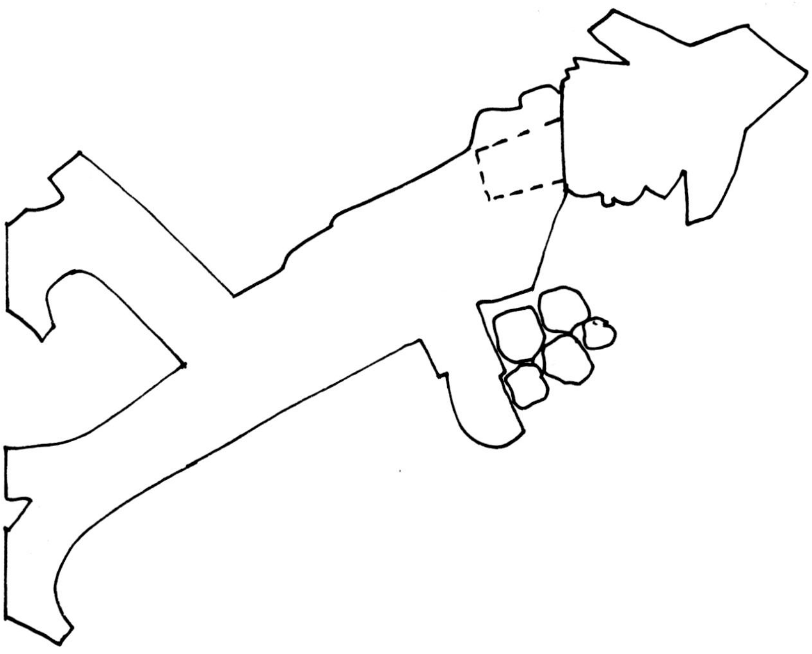

Use small pieces of twig for the firewood. Glue several pieces together. After the cowboy is painted and finished, glue the bundle of firewood in his arms. Mount on a base for stability.

WALKING CAREFULLY #1

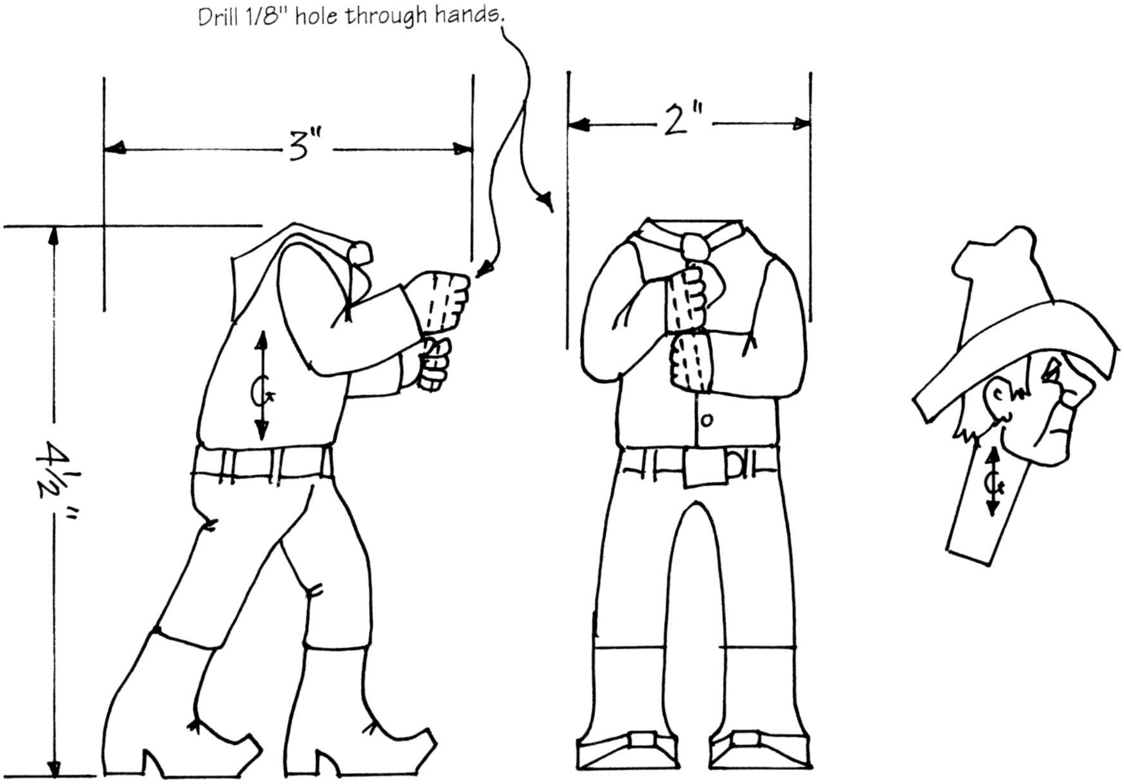

WALKING CAREFULLY #2

After all painting is done, tie a piece of "rope" (refer to TIPS section for information on how to make "rope") around one end of the dynamite box, as shown.

Glue the box in place on the cowboy's back. When the glue is dry, run the loose end of the rope over his shoulder and down through the hole in the hands. Put a small dab of glue in the hole to secure the rope.

Leave a short piece of rope hanging below the hands, and cut off the excess.

Mount on a base for stability.

Make dynamite box from a piece of scrap wood. Dimensions are: 3/4" by 3/4" by 2". Paint box Walnut, then hand letter the word "DYNAMITE" in Black.

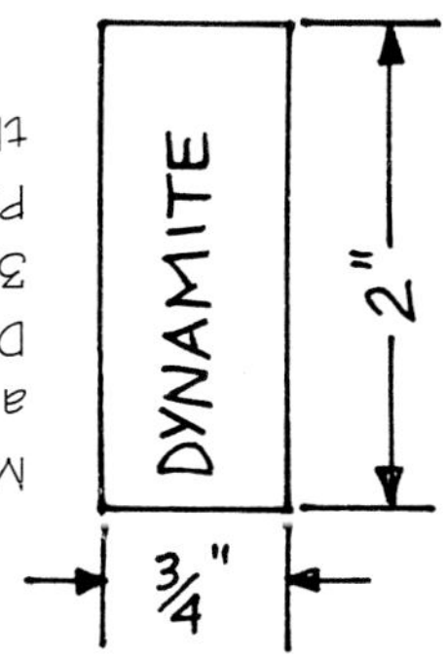

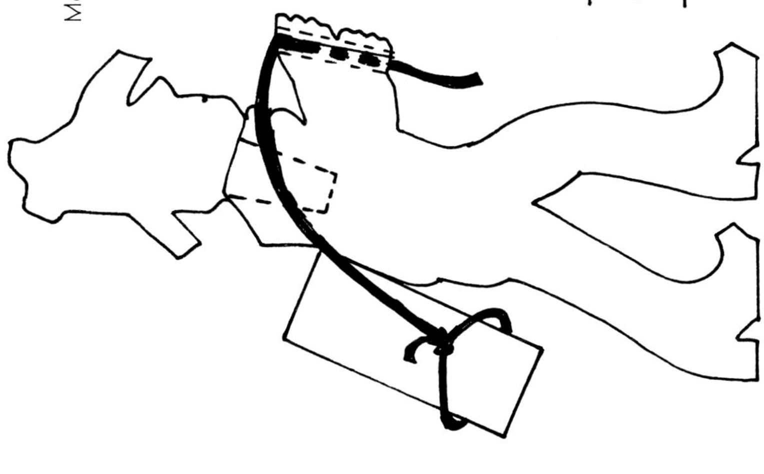

Good Fishing Day #1

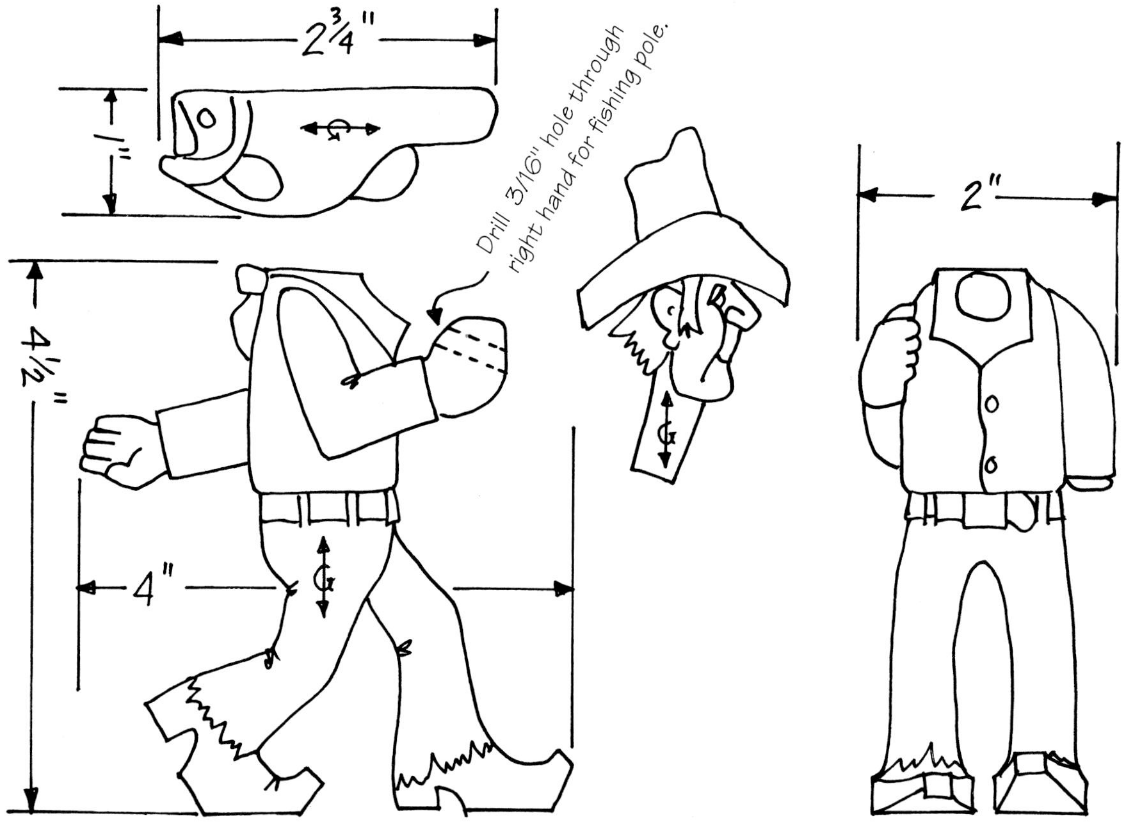

Good Fishing Day #2

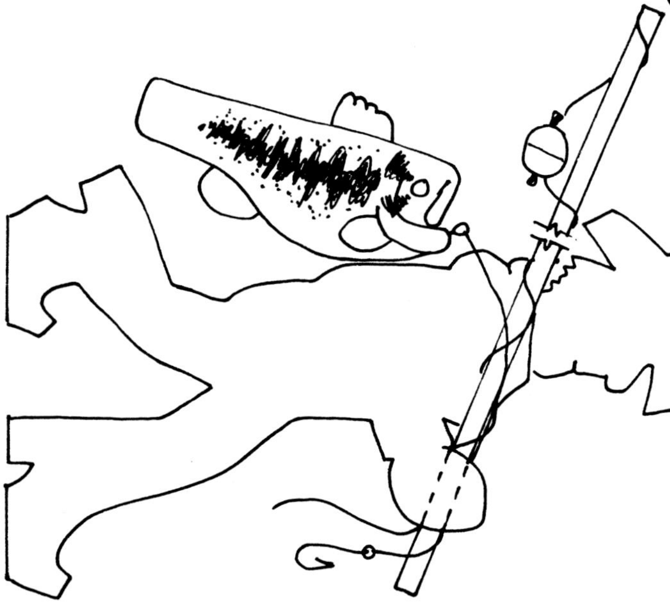

Fishing pole is a section of 3/16" diameter wooden dowel, 6-1/4" long. Bobber is made from scrap wood or an unpainted wooden bead. Paint upper part White, lower part Red. Use heavy Black thread for fishing line. Fashion hook from a scrap piece of wire.

FISH PAINTING DETAILS:
Belly- Pearl White
Upper body- English Yew Green
Eye rays and side splotches- Black
Eye- Walnut Brown with Black Iris

Glue fish to cowboy's back after all painting is done. Run thread from small eyehook in fish mouth, over shoulder and down through hole in hand. Cut to length.

Mount on a base for stability.

I Said Smile! #1

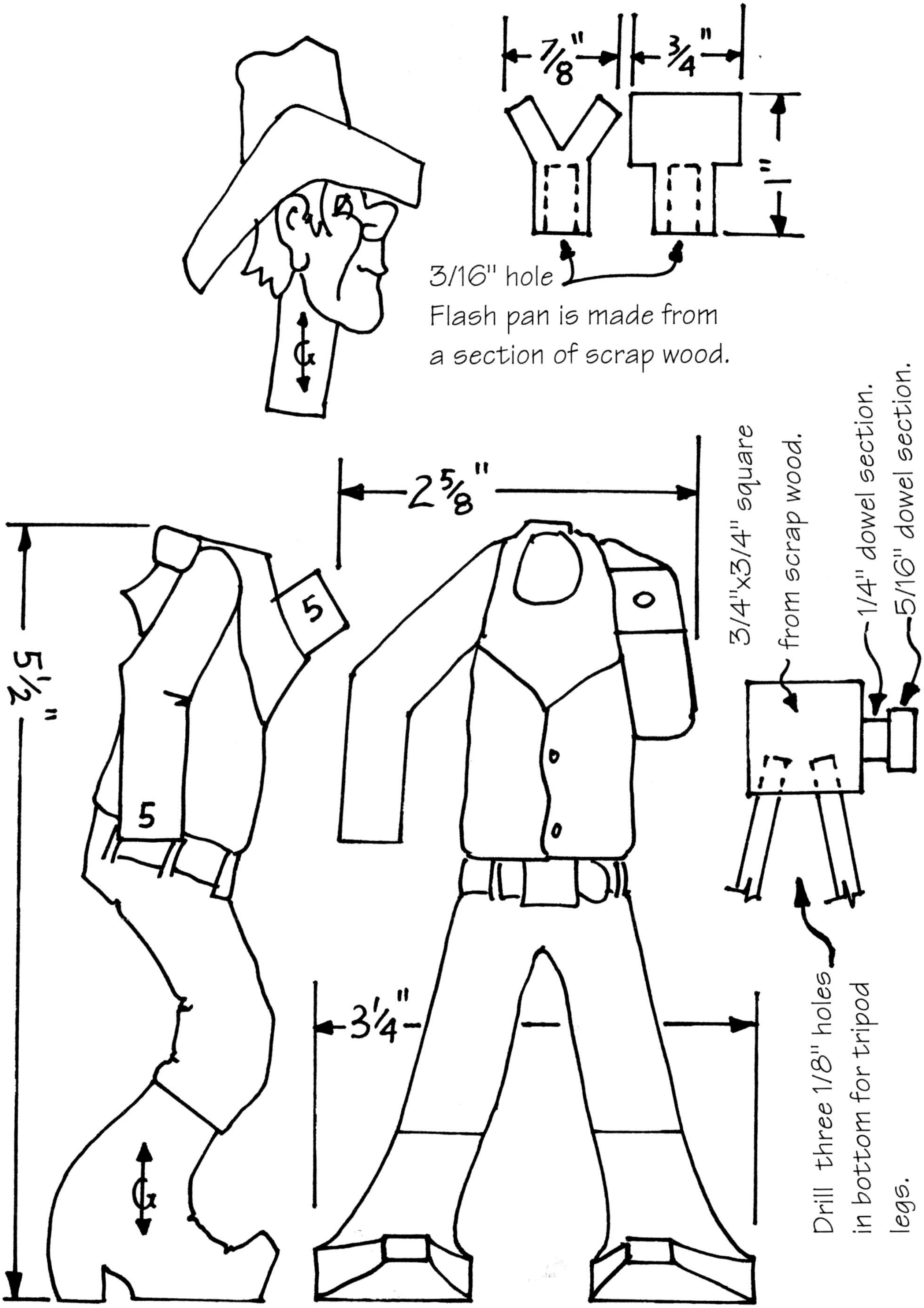

I Said Smile! #2

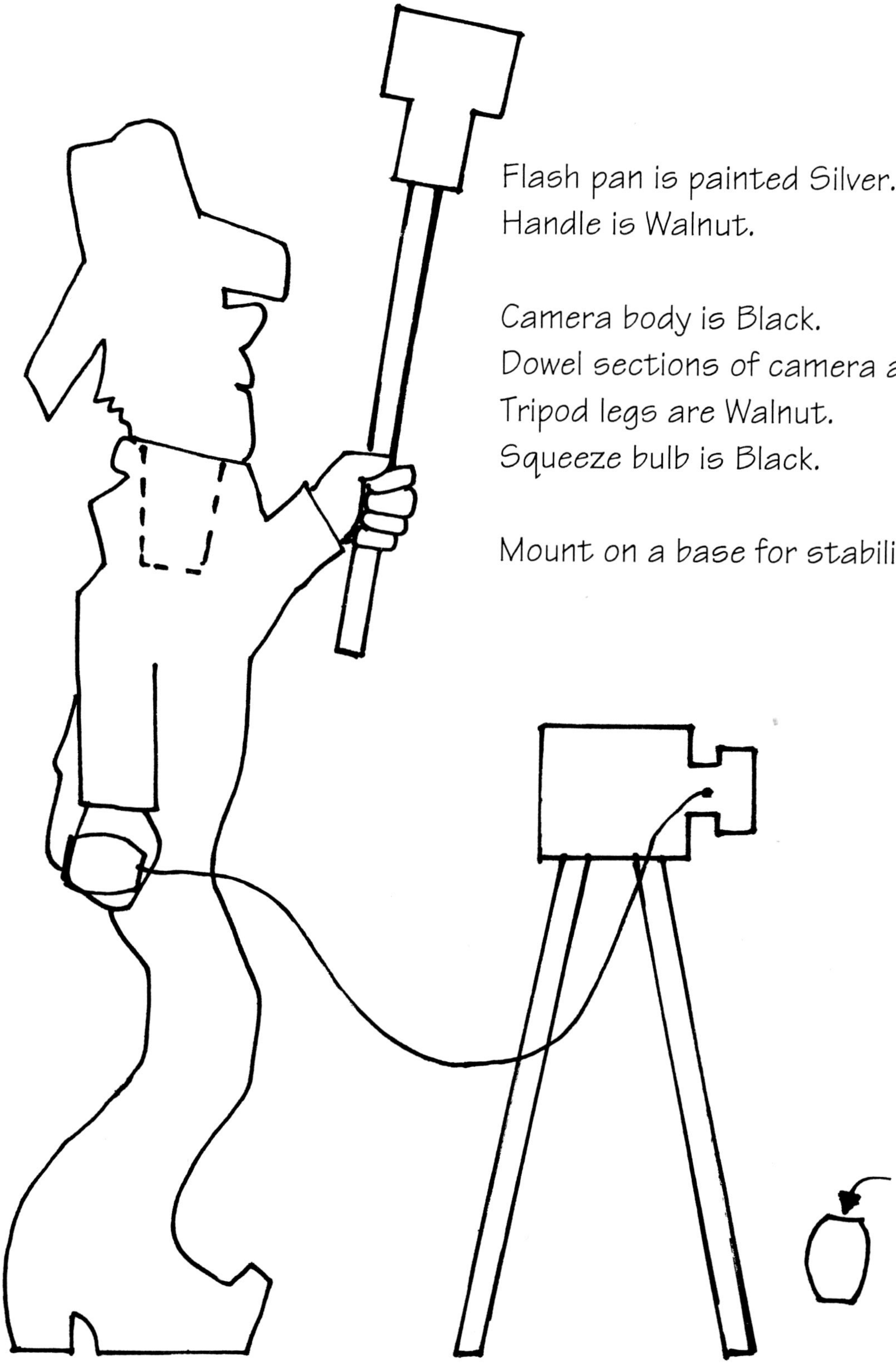

Flash pan is painted Silver.
Handle is Walnut.

Camera body is Black.
Dowel sections of camera are Silver.
Tripod legs are Walnut.
Squeeze bulb is Black.

Mount on a base for stability.

Make squeeze bulb from scrap wood.
Drill small hole in one end of bulb for wire.
Drill small hole in camera for other end of wire.

DAY'S END #1

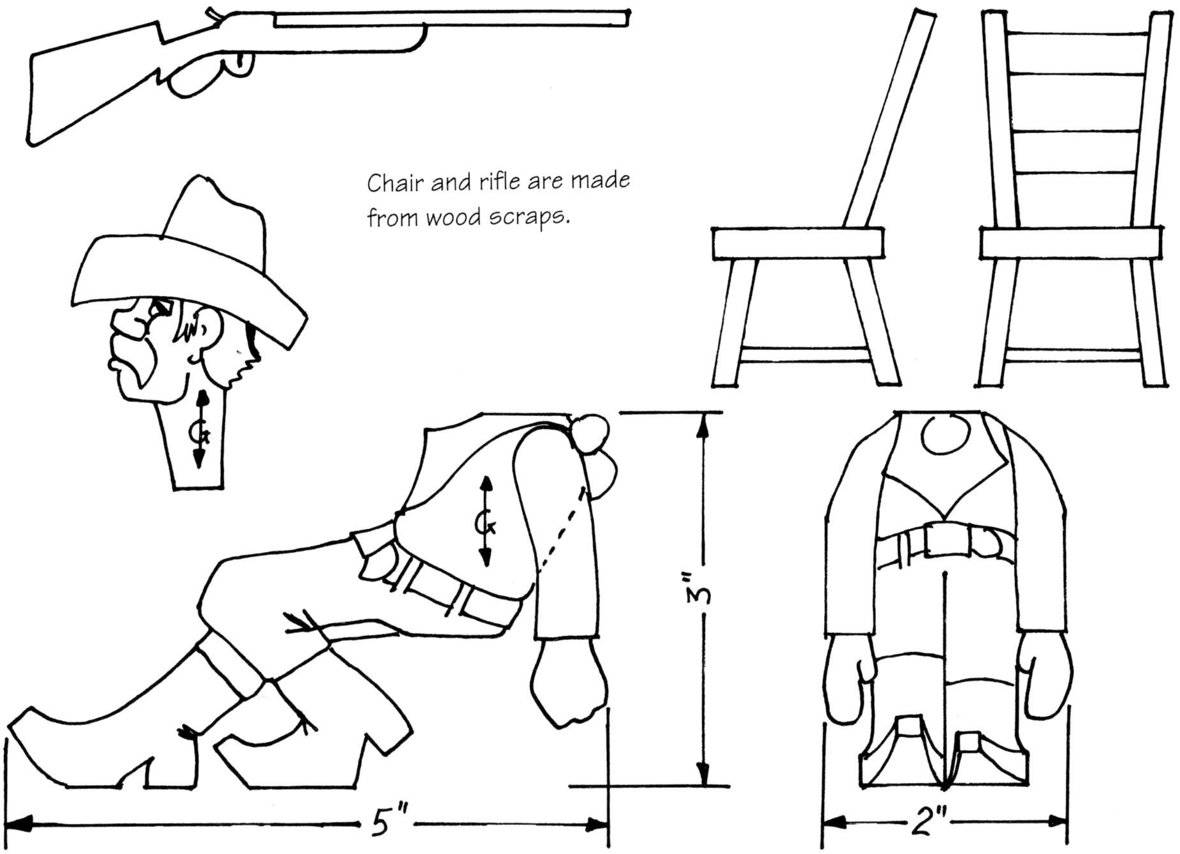

DAY'S END #2

You may position the rifle as shown here, or possibly lean it against the cowboy's leg. (Or, use an arrangement of your choice.)

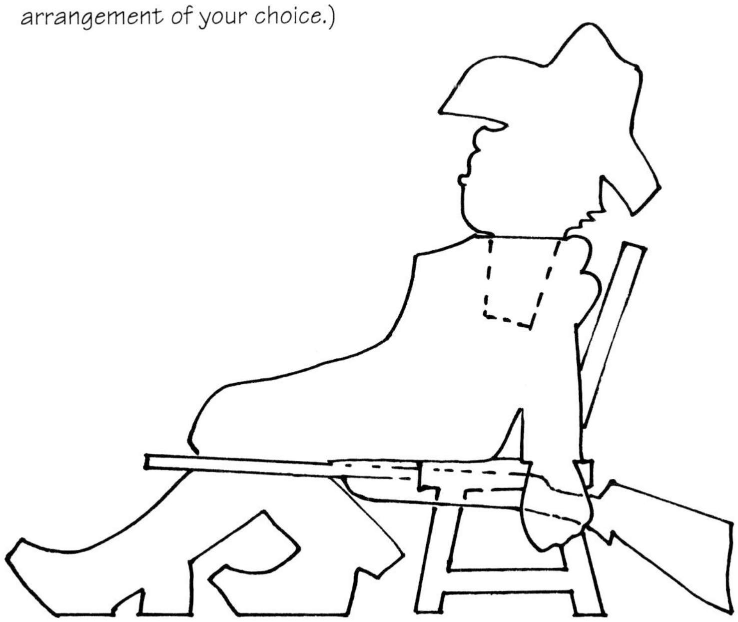

This page must be enlarged 135% for original size.

HAVING A BAD DAY #1

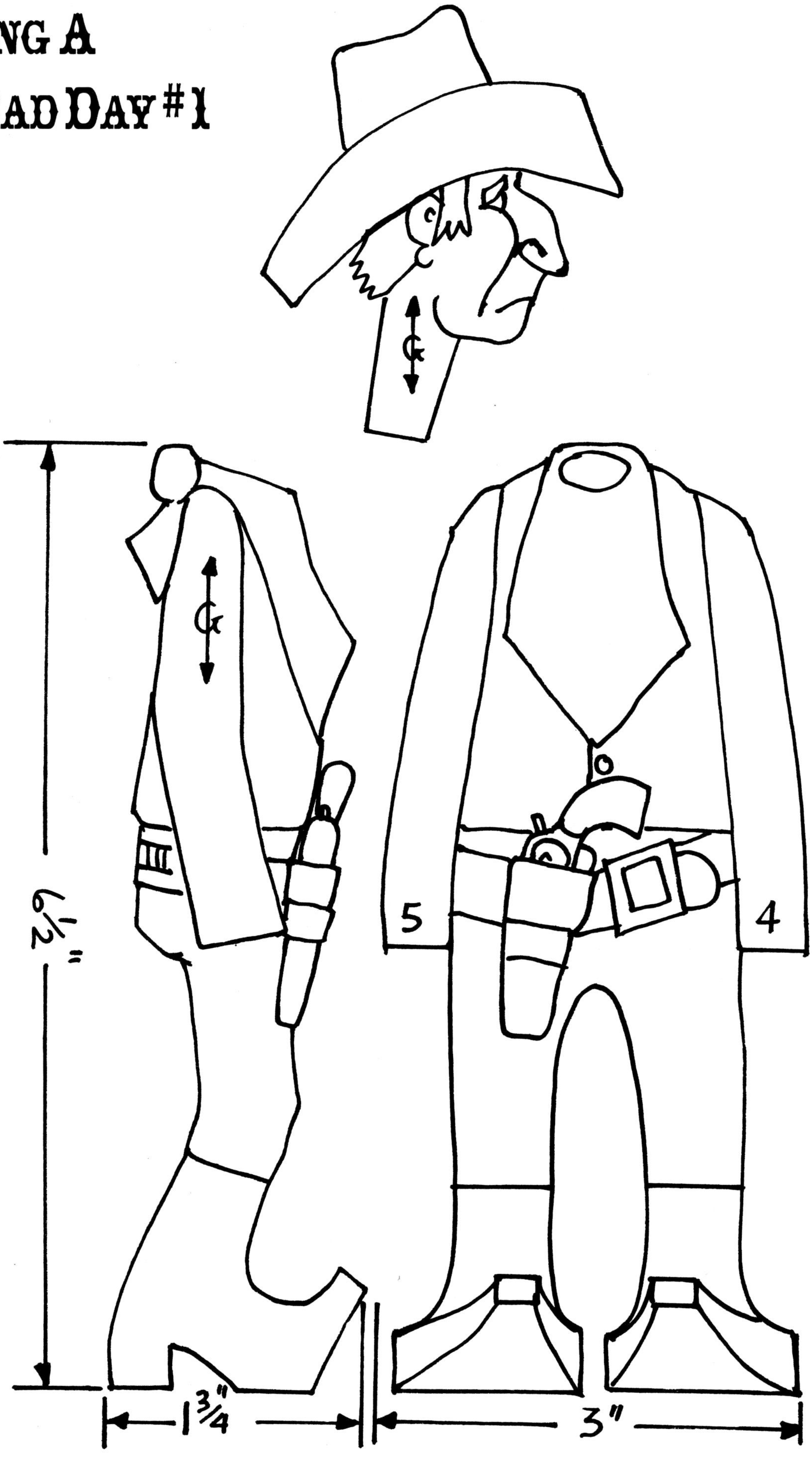

Having A Bad Day #2

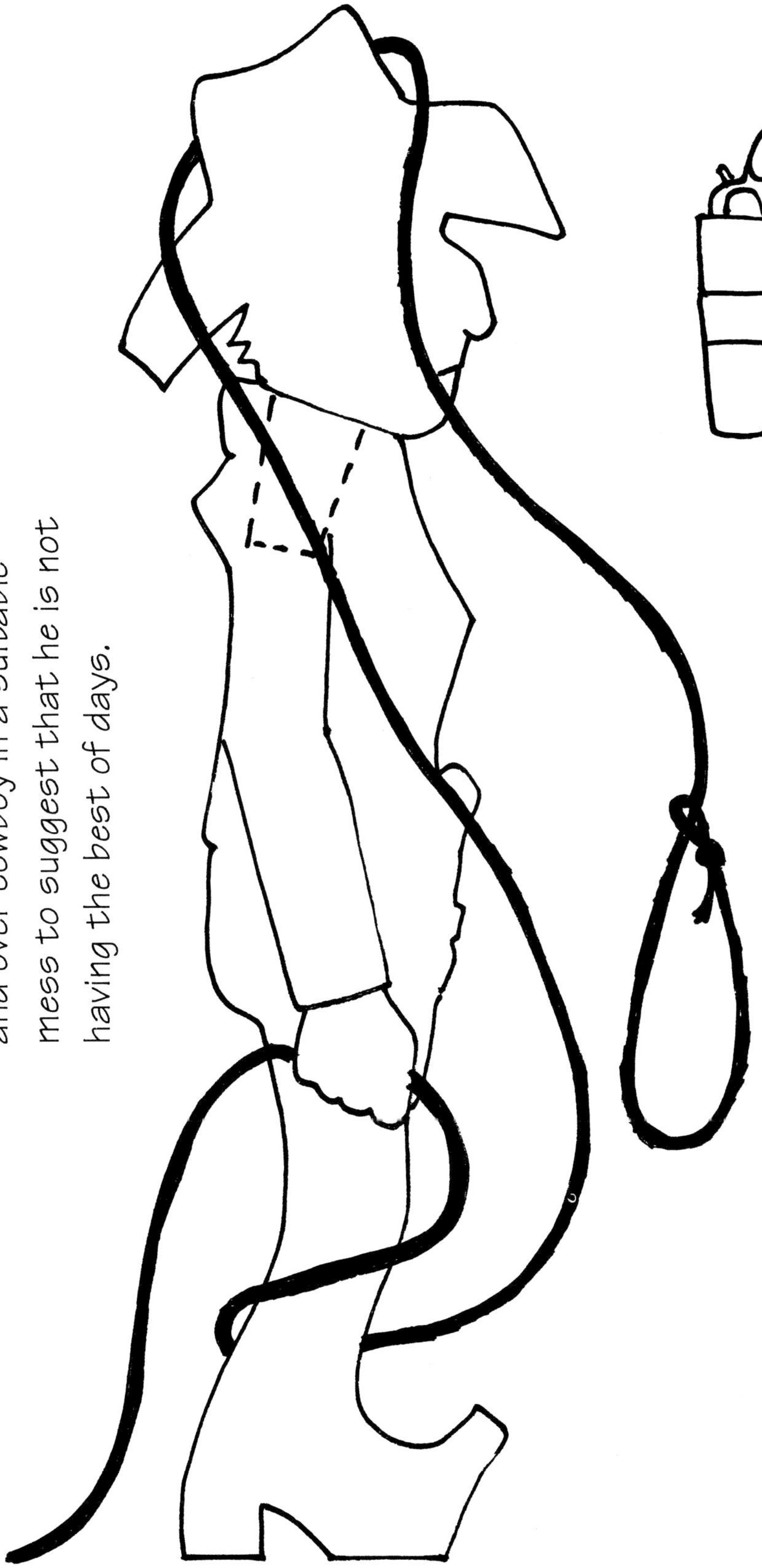

Make rope as described in the TIPS section. Arrange it around and over cowboy in a suitable mess to suggest that he is not having the best of days.

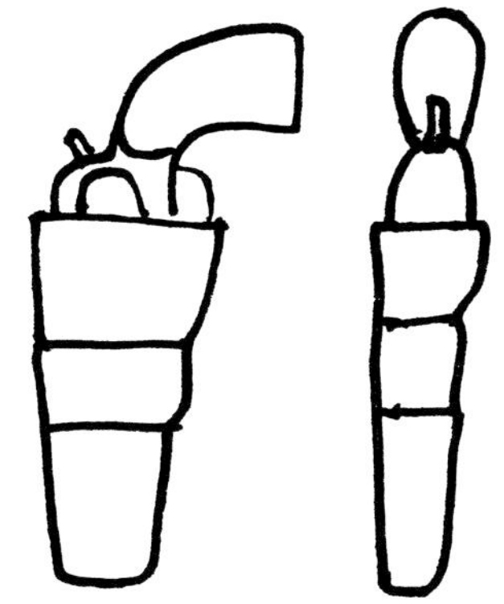

Carve pistol separately and glue in place after all painting is done.

I Could Use Some Help! #1

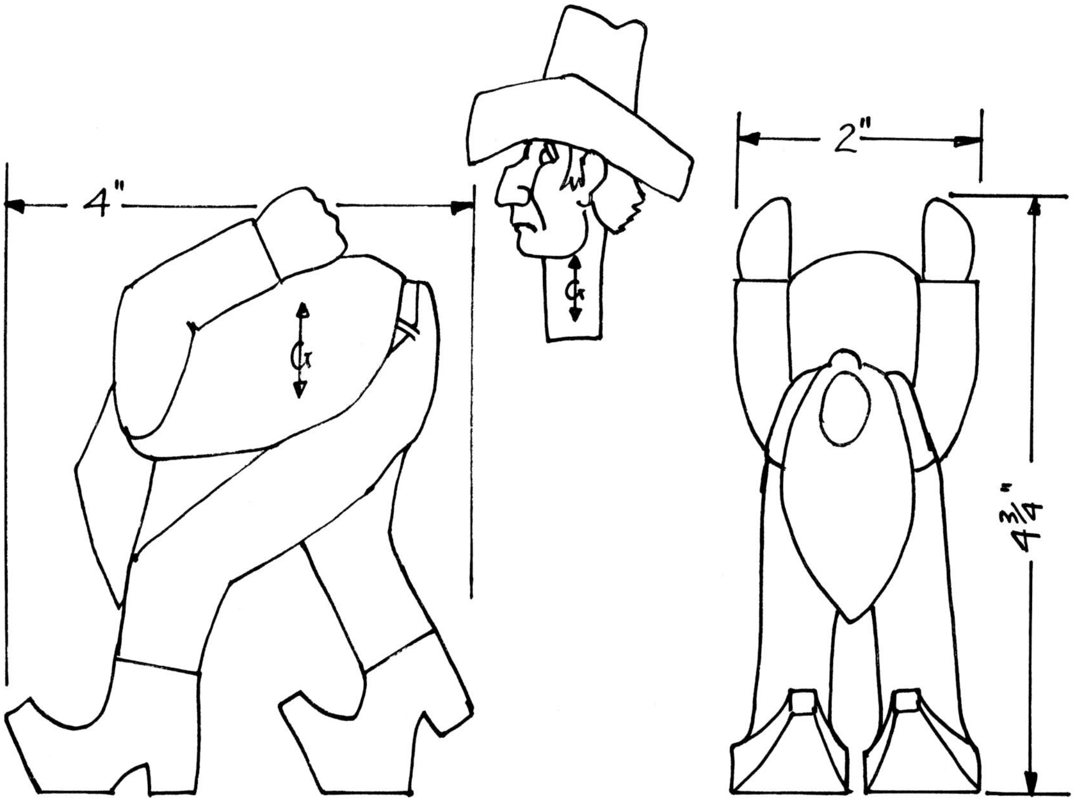

I Could Use Some Help! #2

Nail keg dimensions are approximate. After carving body, measure the inside dimension between the hands. Use this dimension to determine the length of the keg, so it fits properly between the hands. Hand letter the "NAILS" on the side of the keg.

You may want to turn the head to one side to make this guy look more pathetic.

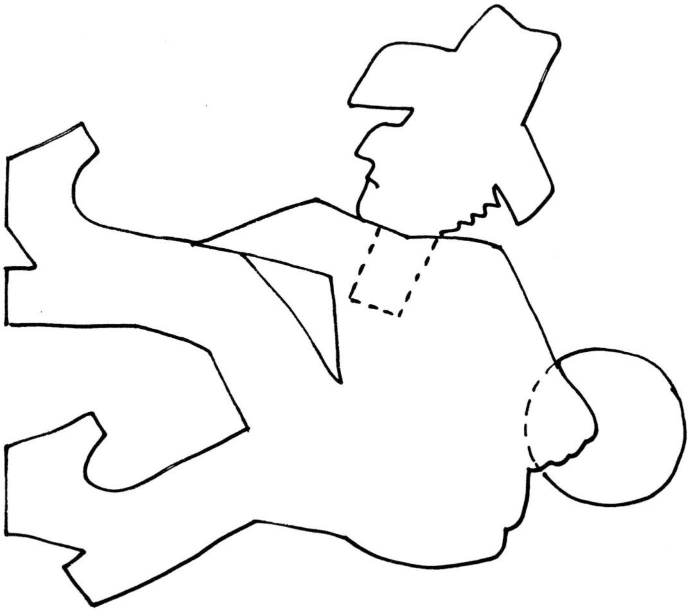

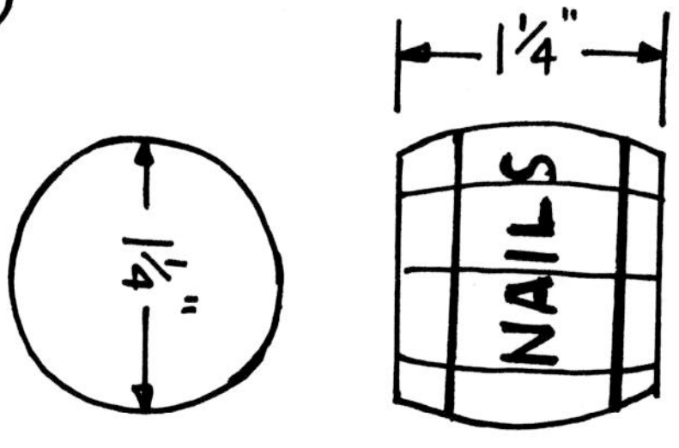

Pages 46 through 48 must be enlarged 135% for original size.

HOLD THAT COW STILL #1

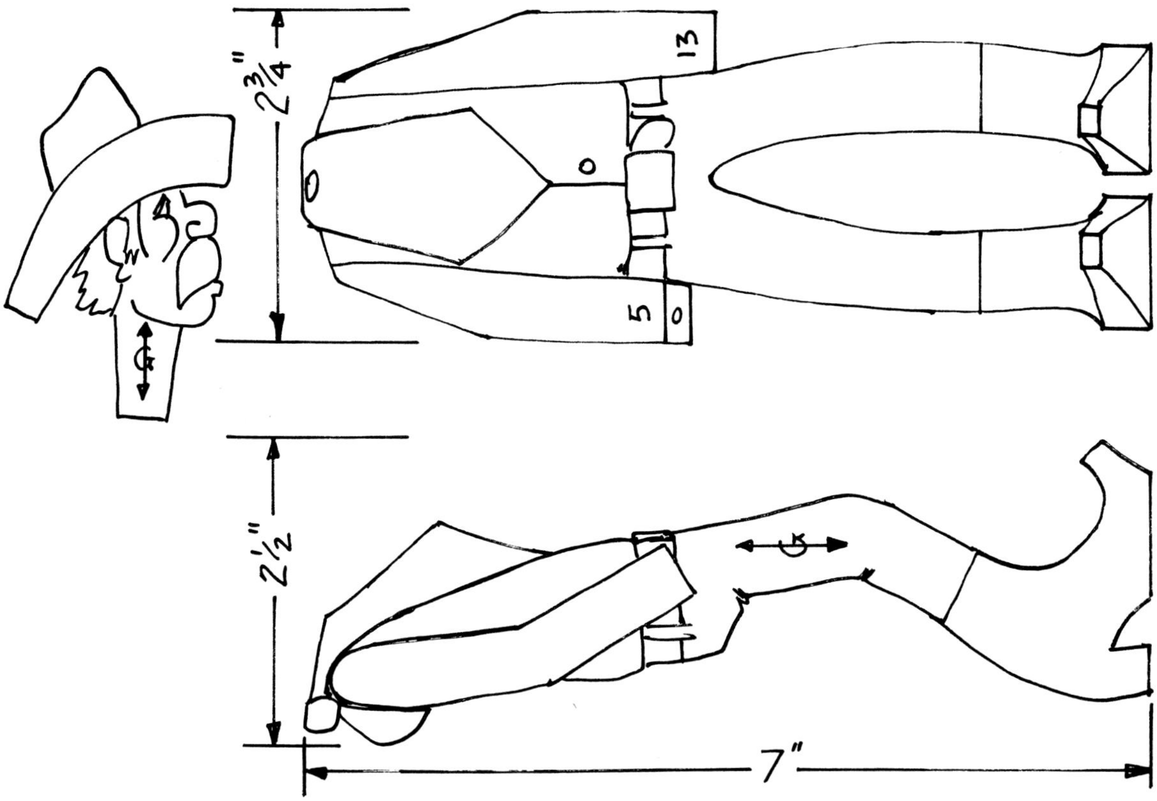

HOLD THAT COW STILL #2

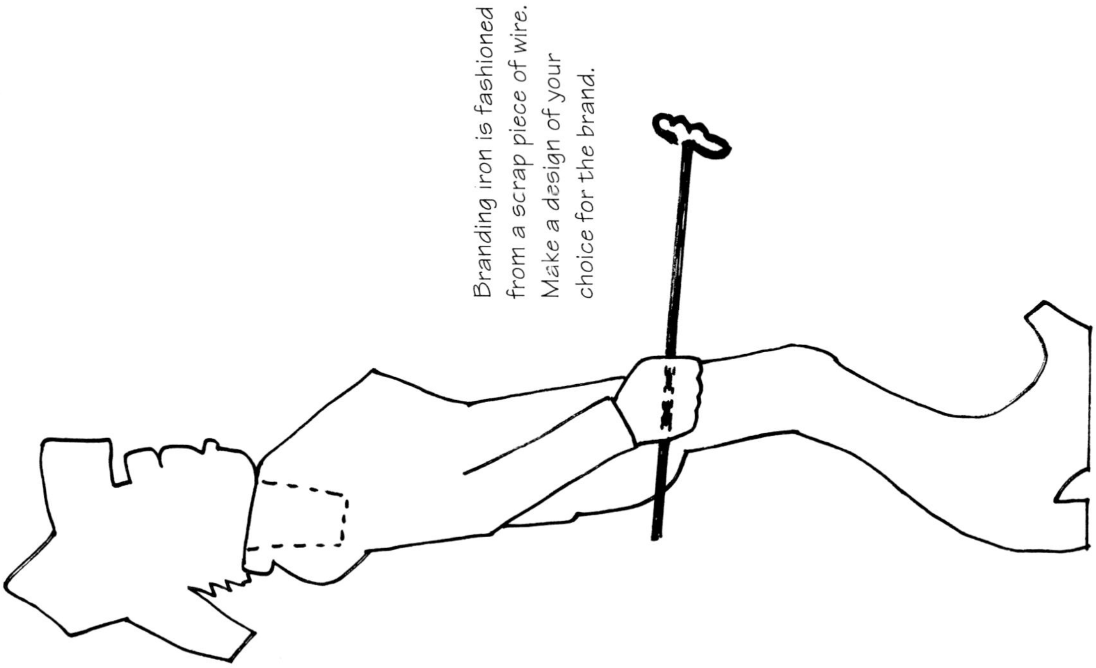

WOOD CHOPPER #1

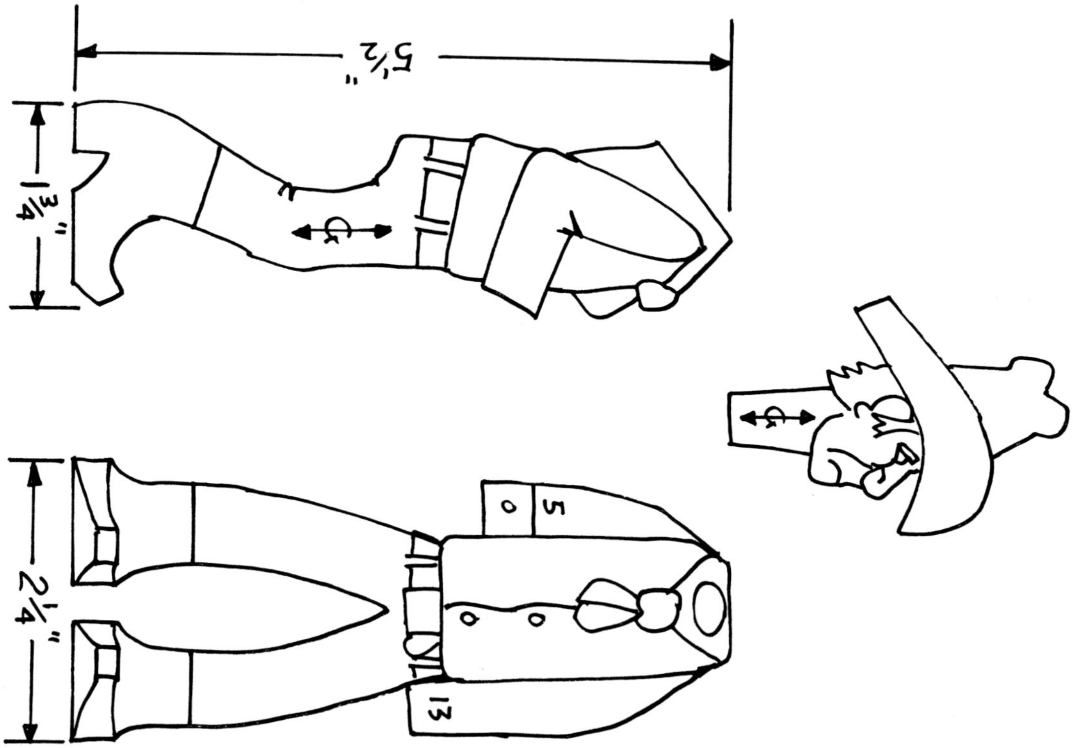

WOOD CHOPPER #2

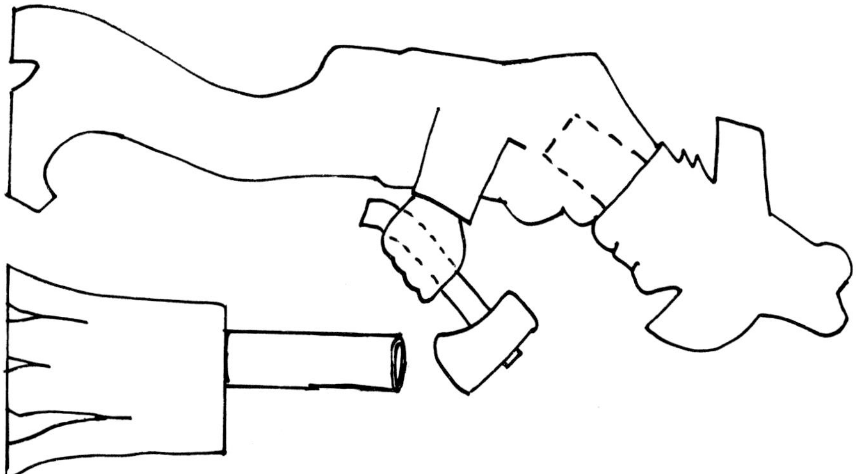

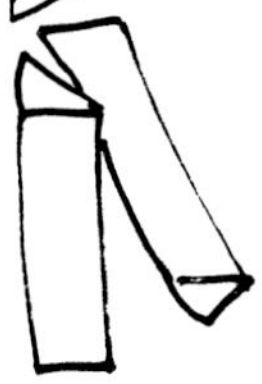

Carve stump from a scrap piece of wood. Use a "V" tool to cut in the root details.

Firewood is made from small twig pieces.

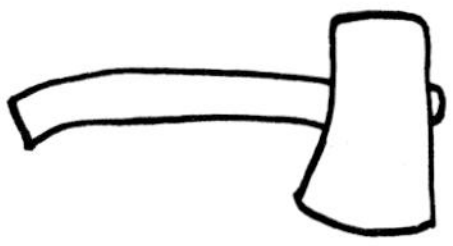

Axe is made from a scrap piece of wood.